Book of our Common Prayer

Andii Bowsher

David,

pray

enjoy

& love !

Andii

Some of the materials have originated elsewhere often from
traditional sources. These have been acknowledged as far as
possible and is fair use and/or explicitly licensed by the originator.
If you further make use of their materials, you should make
appropriate acknowledgement. For other copyrights please see
acknowledgements section at the end of the book. The following
versions of the Bible have been used within the terms of their
copyright licenses.

Cover picture: Joshua K Jackson,
https://unsplash.com/photos/cShfHljtWeA used under terms of
license.

Table of Contents

Contents

Why and how to use this book

In this section you will find some thoughts about how praying in this way could work and is worth considering as part of a Christian pattern of life and prayer. Much of that will be familiar to those who have some experience of being part of church life in churches where there is a definite church year and some kind of tradition which relates to a long history of church. There is also some help understanding why the Lord's prayer is significant and how it is used in the forms of prayer in this book.

Patterned praying and the wider church

The prayers in this book are intended for daily or 'most-days' use. In very broad terms they fit within a long tradition of prayers written and set to assist Christians to pray regularly. The guiding principles in putting these offices together have been two-fold. ("Offices" is a word often used to describe these regular forms of prayer). The chief principle has been to make use of the prayer that Jesus gave to his first disciples in response to the request 'Teach us to pray'. We now usually call that prayer "The Lord's Prayer" though it has also been known as "the Gospel prayer" or often named for it's first phrase, the "Our Father" (in Latin, 'Paternoster' which some English speakers still use). There are slightly different versions of it in the Gospel of Matthew and

1

the Gospel of Luke. Comparing them, we can readily appreciate that there are five phases or movements of prayer covered. Given that there is some variation it is reasonable to suppose that the point is not the exact words but the kinds of things we are being asked to make part of our regular praying.

The second principle informing the shape of these offices has been to include the reading of scripture. For many Christians reading or hearing the Bible regularly is an important discipline, and so it seems important to give room for that in a structure for regular prayer such as this. It seems best to have this component at the start of a time of prayer, perhaps this is because it is the way so many offices model and so much prayer-time advice recommends. In many traditional offices the liturgy around the readings doesn't particularly support the scriptural component in the prayers -at least not explicitly. In the offices in this book, the prayers before and after the readings are intended to prepare us for hearing the scriptures and afterwards to give us forms to respond, if only briefly, to them. There is also a framework for reflection offered. This might be particularly useful if you wanted to use the scripture-centred part of the office separately from the prayer-based second part. One scenario for doing it like that might be to have two times of prayer during the day using one part in each prayer time.

A further principle has been to enable people to pray these offices together with others as well as singly. The offices are designed with a small group praying them in mind. It doesn't have to be that way; a person on their own could pray the office -in fact for me that is the usual way it happens. It does act as a reminder, though, that prayer is envisaged to be a communal activity at heart. After all, the Lord's Prayer itself supposes a community of prayer: "Our Father ... give us... as we forgive..." etc. All of this means that many of the prayers are composed for two or more voices in dialogue and the pronoun 'we' is normal. The default is that one voice would say one part of those prayers and the rest of the voices (whether one or more) would say the other part. Obviously, the person giving voice to the first part could vary, and the 'lead' in that sense could rotate between participants. If you pray this physically alone, simply take both parts yourself. Long experience tells us that it works out fine, just remember, if you do occasionally pray with others, to be aware that you may, in reading on your own, have fallen into habits of speech that need adjusting when sharing the prayers with others and you may want to check whether your prayer partner is expecting you to join in with the responses or not.

The Lord's Prayer structure

The prayer section of the offices (as opposed to the scripture reflection section at the start) is structured around the five kinds of praying that the Lord's Prayer takes us through. Firstly "Our Father in heaven hallowed be your name" is taken to be about praise and thanksgiving; recognition of God's worth and appreciation of God.

Secondly, "your kingdom come, your will be done ..." are taken to be phrases that explain each other. So this kind of praying is about petition and intercession: bringing our concerns to God and seeking alignment with God's own agenda in them.

The third phase takes asking for 'daily bread' to be broadly about bringing our needs before God. These are not just about food but anything that we need to continue living and serving God. The prayers in these sections have often had in mind, Jesus' teaching about our needs particularly as seen in Matthew chapter 6.

In the fourth kind of praying we are invited to be forgiving people as we seek forgiveness. Interestingly, most forms of liturgy seem to have confession of sin and assurance of forgiveness but rarely explicitly include reference to forgiving others. These liturgies always include both dimensions of forgiving and being forgiven.

The fifth and final phrase in the Lord's Prayer is about being led away from situations and circumstances that may overpower us and take us from God's path. The flip side of that is also to orient ourselves to pursuing God's way, following Jesus and keeping in step with the Spirit.

You may wonder about why the final bit of the Lord's Prayer: "Thine is the kingdom" doesn't always get a part in the offices in this book. It's because, in fact, the doxology is not in the original gospel instances of the Lord's Prayer but seems to have been commonly added early on in the history of the first generation or two of Christian communities. So it is treated as optional and only occasionally included in the offices of this book on the basis that it is not properly a part of the Lord's prayer, but rather a devotional extra. When it is included sometimes it is included as it is here, sometimes in another form of doxology

Some background

Many of the existing orders of regular pre-written prayers were developed for and by people in monastic communities. Some have been developed so as to simplify or make them more serviceable for those who live outside of monastic communities -this would include Anglican Morning and Evening Prayer. There have been in history, however, different approaches and we'll come to that a bit further on. Suffice to say for now that many of the most widely available collections of offices are rooted in, or are simply direct copies of, monastic offices.

One of the recurring characteristics of monastic offices is that they are built round saying (or, often, singing or chanting) the Psalms. The Psalms would be set, normally on a rotational basis, and during a normal full day of maybe seven offices, the whole of the book of Psalms would be recited. The nuns or monks would be expected to be praying in the rest of their time in the form of individual devotions and as they worked. They would come together up to seven times a day to recite the Psalms together and this was conceived as joining the prayer of God's people

-which arguably the Psalms are. These gatherings for reciting the Psalms would be accompanied by other prayers and scripture reading.

This is not the only pattern for regularly praying together, that Christians have had. In the church of the first few Christian centuries, lay people would gather for prayer (sometimes called 'Cathedral Offices') where praying together rather than Psalm-recital was the central activity. It is more in the spirit of that tradition that these offices are composed. It should be said here, though, that using the Lord's prayer as a structuring principle for a daily office has not been as common as might be expected if we came to the idea afresh. Probably the lack of uptake for that is that other patterns have preoccupied minds and imaginations. However, I would argue that we should consider giving pride of place to the Lord's Prayer in our regular praying, and if it is right that it was intended to be a basis for regular prayer on the part of the disciples then we should be using it as a basis for a daily office. This book is an attempt to do that with a variety of forms that it is hoped will enable the Lord's Prayer to be explored more fully and to bring fresh insight as the different forms are used.

As you use these offices you would probably become aware that many sentences and phrases in them are actually quotes or paraphrases of passages from the Christian scriptures. Part of the point of this is to help us to pray scripture to some degree. It is something that I have valued about

Anglican liturgies over the years that many of the prayers quote or make use of biblical texts in this we are taking a leaf from Jesus' book for he is depicted in the Gospels as using scripture in reflection and directly in prayer. That said, another aim in composing and compiling the prayers in these offices is to come up with fresh phrases or imagery with the hope that theses may stimulate and enliven our prayers.

The value of regular praying using set prayers.

Many Christians and others would use the word 'liturgy' to mean a sequence of set, pre-written, prayers. I tend to use the word with a broader meaning: for me, liturgy is the way we pattern our time with God. Thinking about it in that way puts a wider variety of ways of praying within the orbit of 'liturgy': For example, a Quiet Time where there is a normal pattern of asking for God's help in reading and understanding Scripture leading into actually reading it, reflecting on it, perhaps learning some of it and then praying out of it, that is a liturgy. It is a pattern of how we might use time put aside to spend with God and with spiritual focus. Even though there is a high degree of extemporisation in the details, the fact that it is a regular sequence (probably with very similar details of the prayers said or thought) means it is a liturgy. Many so-called 'non-liturgical' services of worship are actually often liturgical in the wider sense because they have a fairly predictable pattern to them from the point of view of those who regularly worship. What this means is that we need to think about the value as well as the downsides of using a pattern of set prayers on a regular basis. This is not about liturgy or no-liturgy, but rather content and Christian growth and formation.

Praying with set prayers can be helpful to us. Quite often we can find a phrase in scripture or elsewhere which captures something we would find hard to put into words. Sometimes it can do this in a style or elegance of language we find enticing in prayer and which encourages us to bring ourselves to God with it. Sometimes set prayers can awaken us to ideas of what to praise, thank or ask God for that we probably wouldn't have done by ourselves but which we are glad of as the Spirit enlivens them to us. And then there are the times when our inner life feels dried up or weary and being able to make use of the words that are 'there' is helpful; it's like being able to pray with someone else where they are able to hold us in what we cannot do. It can also be that set prayers enable us to stay focussed or be refocussed at times when our minds might be inclined to wonder.

One objection to set prayers -and therefore to offices of prayer- is that they are not spontaneous. The thought behind this is that only the spontaneous is authentic or genuine and therefore 'honest' before God. Sometimes pre-written prayers can be dismissed as 'vain repetition' -a phrase from Jesus' teaching on prayer and how not to do it. I'd like to address those concerns. First of all with regard to the concern about vain repetition. The phrase comes from the King James' version of Matthew 6:7. Other versions have words like 'heap up words'; 'empty phrases'; 'babble on' and we should note, crucially, that the next bit is to say that this meaningless repetition is like what the heathens /Gentiles /those who don't know God do and they do it because they are trying to make God listen. Jesus' point is that we can be confident God hears us so we don't need to try to impress God. In relation to offices of prayer, this translates to the attitude we have when we pray them: if the set prayers enable us to relate to God, fine; if we use them as a kind of bribe to impress God into listening to us, forget it. We use the forms and the words to help us to focus on God and to carry our desire to connect and to share our concerns and to be touched by God. It needn't replace using our own words, far from it. Using set prayers can support and nurture our own prayers. In fact, in these offices, there is space written in for our own 'of the moment' prayers to be added and included.

In relation to the matter of only spontaneous prayers being authentic and acceptable before God, there are a few things to think more about. One is that Jesus used set prayers or phrases as well as spontaneous ones. For example, "My God, my God, why have you forsaken me" is a quote from Psalm 22:1 -itself a prayer. And noting the use of Psalms - these are hymns and prayers which have been used for centuries by God's people with never a sense of it being wrong to use them as prayers (whether said, sung or inwardly articulated) -this is why they are in the Bible: to be used for praying. This reminds us that using the words of others can be 'authentic' or can stir up within us a real connection with God. It should be noticed, too, that singing hymns and songs to God is praying and it relies on pre-written words so that many can sing together. It is hard to see how, in principle, singing prayers using someone else's words, is different to saying prayers that have been written previously.

Days and seasons

This book has offices for different days and different times and seasons of the year. It's not compulsory, obviously, to use church seasons but many people do find it helpful to change forms every so often and this is one way to do this. Many people also find it good to pray along with the seasons of the church year and so these forms can help us to do that. These orders use imagery and phrases resonant with some of the themes of that season. You'll see that each day has a theme which references a different part of the church's year and there are similarities between these and the seasonal prayers themselves to a greater or lesser extent. There is also an order for 'Everyday' and a 'Pauline' ("Everday -2nd form") form which are intended to be used anytime as an alternative to any of the others.

In addition to what you would expect in terms of seasons of the church year (Advent, Lent, Easter etc), there are some additional orders of prayer for times and seasons and themes which don't often appear -Transfiguration is one and what I have called 'Magnificat' times when we might be reminded of Mary the mother of Jesus -as the name suggests the words of Mary in Luke 1:46ff form a central place in that office. You can also find a 'Pauline Office' which uses phrases from Paul's letters to help us to pray. Creationtide is a new, developing, season in September and up to 4 October. There is an office for "Dark Seasons" which was compiled with winter in higher latitudes in mind when darkness is a bigger part of everyday experience and it uses imagery of dark and light to draw on that experience as we pray.

There are also some 'bedtime' offices -'Night Prayer'. Having a short office before bed is something that has grown in popularity in recent years and so these draw on some of the traditional prayers and imagery for Compline (the traditional late night office) but restructure them in Lord's Prayer format. One of the constants in these offices is the use of the Nunc Dimittis -the Song of Simeon from Luke 2. In these orders of prayer, the Nunc Dimittis is used to round off a time of thankful reflection on the day past rather than as a response to the scripture reading. These night prayer offices are not written 'seasonally' but simply with some variety to be used as you find helpful.

Praying offices more than once a day?

If you are looking to pray an office more than once a day and would like to use these liturgies but would also prefer not to pray the same one twice a day, then (assuming that you don't count the night prayers) I suggest the following. It could work to use a seasonal one and a day-of-the-week one. So in early December you might pray the Advent office in the mornings but the days' offices of the relevant day in the afternoon. Or in times outside of the seasons (so called 'ordinary time') you might consider the days' prayers in the mornings and use one of the Everyday forms on your second sitting.

Using this book

This book doesn't contain all that you might want to pray. You will also want to have access to a Bible. You might also wish either to annotate this book or have a notebook for prayer materials you want to bring to your regular prayer. You may find too that using bookmarks or sticky notes might also help you to travel back and forth. It is intended to be something of a working book, and so annotations and aids are to be encouraged.

When it comes to the scripture readings, you are, of course, free to tackle that in whatever way makes sense to you in your circumstances. Many people use a Bible reading plan or a lectionary[1] which gives you a series of readings on a daily basis. If you don't have either of these, you might want to make provision by some other means to have biblical material for that part of the office. It's also possible that you might have bible reading notes. In compiling these offices, I had in mind the possibility of people using a variety of bible reading schemes and devotional notes. There are plenty available on line if you wish to investigate further. It is really up to you.

In some of the liturgies you will see the word "Collect". A Collect is simply a prayer of a few lines which aim to collect our attention together around a particular theme. They tend to vary for occasions and seasons. Many churches which use a lectionary tend to print a collect for the week each Sunday. If you don't have access to a lectionary with Collects or a notice sheet with a collect, there are a dozen towards the back of this book. Alternatively, simply leave it out or have a moment of quiet to 'collect' your thoughts.

Conventions for type-styles used

Italics are used for things that are not meant to be said out loud but rather are to help use the time and the prayers or to indicate where something has come from.
Bold is used when words are meant to be said together.
Emboldened italics tend to indicate a title of a canticle or similar.
Ordinary type is for things that the person who is

leading at that point says on their own.

Three little dots like this … are shorthand to suggest a time of quiet or reflection. Normally the person leading at that point would be responsible for moving on to the next part after a suitable period of time.

Days of the week

In this section of the book there is an order of service for each day of the week as well as an 'Everyday' prayer which could be used on any day of the week. Most of the days have a thematic link relating to some of the themes of salvation and traditional seasons of the Church's year.

Sunday

Sunday's prayers reflect the traditional idea of Sunday as a day when we commemorate Jesus' rising from death. Of course, in the Hebrew and Christian traditions, Sunday is the first day of the week. For Christians this is a mark of the idea that 'the eighth day' represents the recreation, the New Creation inaugurated by the Resurrection.

Source of all life, as a child to her mother:
We turn to you
Saviour of all life, as music to song:
We turn to you.
Sustainer of all life, as a flower towards the sun:
We turn to you.

> *The Psalm[s] …*
> *Reader, announcing each reading:*

Let us attend; words of life in [*passage is announced*] ….

> *Collect and readings*
> *Reader or service leader, after the readings:*

Here ends the reading.
Here begins its outworking.

> *There may be a time of quiet and/or shared reflection. A Framework(p.139) for reflection, may be used.*
> *… A Canticle may be said*

Let us respond to the questions Jesus asked of Peter.
Do you Love me?

Lord, you know that I love you.
Jesus said: Tend my sheep. And, Follow me.

... A few moments to respond inwardly

Amen.
Amen

....

Blessèd are you, God, redeemer and life-giver;
to you be glory and praise for ever!
In the beginning, you spoke the world into being
from the unformed emptiness. In Christ you spoke
the Word of life into the unmaking void of death,
raising your Life from death and enfolding us in that
victory. God of new and eternal life:
Hallowed be your name
We ask for God's eternal-life-giving to be known in
our world, saying: Living God:
glorify your name

*Concerns for the world and its people are brought
before God, at this point closing with the series of
one-line responses below.*

In this world of sin and death, and yet of blessings
and common grace; Living God:
glorify your name.
In our world's global community, in our world's living
systems;   Living God:
glorify **your name.**
In your church as we proclaim your new life in
thought and word and deed;   Living God:
glorify your name.
Among all whose lives our lives touch, friends,

colleagues and families;   Living God:
glorify your name.
In our laughter, and tears, in our fear and our hope;
Living God:
glorify your name.
In our needs and weakness in our provision and
supply;   Living God:
glorify your name

Rewritten from a prayer in
Patterns of Worship, 1995

God of Life in all its fullness, we come to you in
sorrow for our sins, and confess to you our
weaknesses and unbelief.

Recollection of what we need to confess.

We have lived within the horizons of this life alone,
failing to take our bearings from eternal Life.
Merciful God, forgive us.
And restore us to life.
We have laid others in the tomb of our
unforgiveness, withholding the word of life.
Forgive us, Merciful God
And restore us to life-giving.
Let us attend; Christ breathes upon us the peace
and forgiveness of God.

...a moment for quiet reflection on our
forgiveness....

Who will rescue us from this body of death?
Thanks be to God through Jesus Christ our
Lord!

As we seek to forge a new future living the new life of Christ let us reflect on what the coming hours may bring, and pause to recognise the unexpected and unforeseeable will be part of our future.

...

When temptation seems to entomb us,
Roll away the stone.
When our values seem tested to destruction
Raise our hopes to new life.
When good and right ways ahead seem closed,
Help us to find your way through.
When we go forward expecting to anoint the dead
Surprise us with your Life.
When we walk in the old order of sin and death
Walk beside us, remind us of your purposes and reveal yourself to us afresh.
You have created us in Christ for good,
Help us to walk the paths you have prepared for us.

Monday

Many of Monday's prayers pick up the themes of creation and the Holy Spirit.

How lovely is your dwelling place O Lord Almighty!
My soul longs, even faints for the courts of the Lord.
My heart and my flesh cry out for the living God.

...

Who is it that we seek?
We seek God: Sender, Sent and Sending.
Let's seek God with all our heart
Amen. God be our centre.
Let's seek God with all our soul
Amen. God be our vision.
Let's seek God with all our mind
Amen. God be our wisdom.
Let's seek God with all our strength
Amen. God be our souls' shelter.

...

God, by your Spirit, move over the face of our hearts
and minds.
bring order to our decisions, enliven our attitudes
 and enlighten our thinking; enticing reflection
towards your Wisdom

...

Reader: Let us listen for the word of life.

> *Psalms and readings are announced and read.*
> *When all have been read:*

Reader: God has sent forth the word
May it not return empty.

A framework for reflection (p.139) may be used..

...

The following Canticle may be said or some other

**You take us from the nations,
you gather us from every land,
You sprinkle clean water upon us,
and wash us from all our uncleannesses,
as from all our idols you cleanse us.
A new heart you give us,
a new spirit you put within us.
You remove from our body the heart of stone
and give a heart of flesh.
we are your people,
and you are our God.**

based on Ezekiel 36.24-26,28b

**Hallowed be your name, Father, through the Son
in the Holy Spirit;
as in the beginning, so now and for ever. Amen.**

A collect may be said.

...

Everliving God, the heavens declare your praise and
yet cannot contain your glory. May your name be
kept holy in our heartfelt praise.

*...Prayers and/or songs of praise and thanks may
be shared here...*

Blessèd are you, creator God;
to you be glory and praise for ever!
Your Spirit hovered over the unformed creation, and
overshadowed Mary as the Christ was enwombed,
and now your Holy Spirit flares up among us

assuring that we are your children, intimating to us your delight in us,
Our God In heaven, father and mother to us:
Hallowed be your name!
Creator God, release your Spirit to brood over the desolations of human society; deformed by discordant voices, and decentred by competing desires.
Let there be justice,
let there be peace
and let there be healing

> *… prayers or biddings relating to these themes may be added here the leader ending with:*

Send forth your Spirit:
And renew the face of the earth.

Everliving Lover of our souls, you draw all people to yourself, wooing us Spirit to spirit. We remember before you the work of the gospel as it goes forth not to return empty.

> *… prayers or biddings relating to this topic may be added here. The leader ends this* section with:

Send forth your Spirit:
And renew the face of the earth.

> …

Passionately faithful God; may the eternal flame of your Spirit burn in our souls and warm the lives of those whose lives we touch in person, process or in prayer.

...prayers or biddings relating to this topic may be added here the leader ending with

Send forth your Spirit:
And renew the face of the earth.

...

Be the wind in the sails of our lives and as we are
blown forward by your Spirit may we know your
comfort and provision

...requests for God's provision may be added here the leader ending with

Send forth your Spirit:
And renew the face of the earth.

...

There have been times when we have quenched
your Spirit in our self-serving or grudge-bearing

...

We ask your help so that we might truly repent
and know
and offer
joyful forgiveness,

...

Blow upon us your peace-making breeze:
And renew the face of our lives.
Let us attend; Christ breathes upon us the peace
and forgiveness of God.

a moment for quiet reflection on our forgiveness.

Father may your Spirit overshadow us in all that
tests us: do not let us fall away from you.

When we are becalmed
blow us forward into your purposes.
If we grow cold towards your Reign and
righteousness,
Rekindle your love in our spirits.
If we find ourselves tested in a dry place,
Water our souls.
In our living of this day:
**yours be the kingdom, the power and the glory,
for ever and ever. Amen.**

Tuesday

Tuesday's prayers tend to reflect the themes of Christ's
return and the consummation of creation at the End of all
things.

I will listen to what the Lord God will say
for God shall speak peace to his people
to the faithful shall God speak
that they do not turn again to folly

From Psalm 85:8

> *...Pause to recognise God's presence.*

My soul faints with longing for your salvation,
and in your word have I put my hope.

> *Collects, Psalm(s) and readings. When they have*
> *been read*
>
> ...

The word that goes out from God's mouth
shall not return empty,
it shall accomplish God's purpose,
and succeed in what it is sent to do.

> *reflection silently and/or together out loud. A*
> *framework for reflection is (p.139).*

> *The following Canticle may be said or some other*

Blessed are you, Lord God of Israel;
you have come to your people and set us free.
You have raised up for us a mighty Saviour,
born of the house of your servant David.
Through your holy prophets you promised of old

to save us from our enemies,
from the hands of all who hate us;
to show mercy to our forebears
and to remember your holy covenant.
This was the oath you swore to our father
Abraham:
to set us free from the hands of our enemies,
free to worship you without fear,
holy and righteous before you,
all the days of our life.
In your tender compassion, O God
the dawn from on high shall break upon us,
to shine on those who dwell in darkness and the
shadow of death,
and to guide our feet into the way of peace.

*Based on the ELLC version of the
Song of Zachariah.*

O Lord, open our lips
And our mouth shall proclaim your praise.
We have waited on your loving-kindness, O God,
in the midst of your temple.
As with your name, O God,
so your praise reaches to the ends of the earth;
your right hand is full of justice.
Hallowed be your name!

*… when any further expressions of praise and
thanks have been shared:*

Sovereign Lord, our End as our Beginning, In your
compassion, your dawn from on high scatters the
deathly shades haunting our darknesses: Our God in
heaven, father and mother to us:
Hallowed be your name

...

Bring in your Reign, O God
Let Godly hopes prevail.
A day is coming and has already come when all
good hopes will blossom and wickedness will die
back never to be remembered
Just and merciful God, hasten that Day and in this
age give us a foretaste of your kingdom: Bring in
your Reign, O God
Let Godly hopes prevail.

> *Concerns and biddings for the good of the world
> and God's desires may be mentioned here or
> after each or all of the following petitions*

In that day, death and mourning, crying and pain will
be no more
and God will wipe away every tear.
Bring in your Reign, O God
Let Godly hopes prevail.
In that Day, of the increase of Christ's government
and peace there shall be no end.
Bring in your Reign, O God
Let Godly hopes prevail.
In that Day, your Spirit will fill all things and all shall
know you.
Bring in your Reign, O God
Let Godly hopes prevail.

As we walk the path of your Dream of a healed
creation, may we know your hand supplying our
needs.

> *... recalling of needs in silence or aloud*

As we ask for daily bread,

Bring in your Reign, O God
Let Godly hopes prevail.

...

Give us this day the courage and insight to forgive others:
as you forgive us our trespasses...

> *A moment of silence for recollection and response to this call ...*

in our forgiving and being forgiven:
Bring in your Reign, O God
Let Godly hopes prevail.

...

As we seek to forge a new future living the new life of Christ, let us reflect on what challenges to our faithfulness and integrity the coming hours may bring, and pause before the many unknowns of our future

...

When we are tested by temptation
strengthen us.
when our commitment to your Love is put to trial,
save us.
When evil ensnares
free us.
For yours is the kingdom, the power and the glory,
now and forever. Amen.

Wednesday

Wednesday's prayers tend to reflect the theme of Christ's incarnation.

O God open our souls
to awaken to your presence
O God open our minds
to hear your call
O God open our hearts
to know your love
O God open our lives
to be fully alive in you and to our neighbour.

> *... A Collect may be said.*

As we hear the scriptures read, may they lead us to the Christ and may we find in Jesus the fulfilment of all our searching.

> *Psalm(s) and readings.*

Blessed are those who hear the word of God
And obey it.

> *There may be a time of quiet and/or shared reflection. A framework for reflection, (p.139) may be used.*
>
> *When readings and reflection are done, the following Canticle may be said or some other*

My **soul proclaims your greatness O Lord;
my spirit rejoices in you O God our Saviour,
You have looked with favour on your lowly
servant.**

From this day all generations will call us blessed:
Almighty, you have done great things for us, and holy is your name.
You have mercy on those who fear you from generation to generation.
You have shown strength with your arm and scattered the proud in their conceit, casting down the mighty from their thrones and lifting up the lowly.
You have filled the hungry with good things, and sent the rich away empty.
You have come to the help of your servant Israel, remembering your promise of mercy, the promise made to our forebears, to Abraham and his children forever.

Based on ELLC translation of
Luke 1:46-55

...

Glory to God in the highest:
and on earth -peace and goodwill.
Holy, holy holy, Lord, God of power and might.
Heaven and earth are full of your glory,
Hosanna in the highest!

...expressions of of praise and thanks ...

O God, you have done great things for us
And holy is your name.

...

Your heavenly will be done in all created beings!
May your commonwealth of peace and freedom
sustain our hope and come on earth.
Father, may your will be fleshed out:

on earth as in heaven.

Concerns and biddings for the good of the world and for God's agenda may be mentioned here or after the following petitions….

Your will is for the liberation of creation in bondage to decay
Father, may your will be be fleshed out:
on earth as in heaven.
Your will is for peace and justice
Father, may your will be be fleshed out:
on earth as in heaven.
Your will is for all to come to a knowledge of salvation
Father, may your will be be fleshed out:
on earth as in heaven.

Concerns and biddings for the good of the world and God's desires might be mentioned here if they haven't been before.

With the bread we need for today, feed us.
Into what will sustain our life in you, lead us.

… reflection and requests for daily bread and provision.

We look to you to supply our need. Be our provider and strength.
Father, may your will be be fleshed out:
on earth as in heaven.

,,,

Forgiving God, we have held onto your gifts and stayed aloof.

…

God forgive us

31

And Let grace live within us

Sharing God; we have resisted your life within us.

...

God forgive us
And Let grace live within us

...

God who first loved us, help us to love others by
forgiving.

...

God forgive us
And Let grace live within us

> *There may be silence to reflect on forgiving. After
> an appropriate interval, words of forgiveness may
> be said.*

As we seek to live embodying the values and
commitments of God's just and gentle Rule, let us
reflect on challenges to our faithfulness and integrity
that we are likely to face in the coming hours, and
let's recognise our future has many unknowns to
wrongfoot us.

...

We are called to bear Christ into our world. With
Mary we ask, how can this be?

...

We take to heart the Angel's reply:
The power of the Most High will overshadow you;
with God it is possible:
Let it be to us according to your Word.

Thursday

Thursday's prayers tend to reflect the theme of the season of Epiphany: Christ's revelation to the world and fulfilment of the desires of the ages, represented in the visit of the Magi, along with recalling Christ's Baptism and the changing of water into wine.

Let us pray that the flame of God's loving presence may spring up in our hearts and transform us by the knowledge of divine glory.

A light may be lit as the following prayer is said:

We take refuge in the Divine Light,
The Flame of Truth
The soul's Ray
We take refuge in the Embodiment of Glory
The Lamp of our path
The Essence of love

Based on a prayer from the
Church of South India

...

As we hear the scriptures read, may they lead us to the Christ. And may we find in Jesus the fulfilment of all our searching.

Collects, Psalm(s) and readings. There may be a time of quiet and/or shared reflection. A framework for reflection(p.139) may be used. When the readings and reflection are finished...

Blessed are those who hear the word of God
And do it.
Jesus calls us to continue to follow him.

...

Lord Christ Jesus, we hear your call.
To whom shall we go? You have the words of
eternal life.
**We believe and know you are the Holy One of
God.**

...

The following Canticle may be said or some other

**Now, Lord, you let your servant go in peace:
your word has been fulfilled.
My own eyes have seen the salvation
which you have prepared in the sight of every
people:
a light to reveal you to the nations
and the glory of your people Israel.**

ELLC version of Luke 2:29-32

**Hallowed be your name, Father, through the Son
in the Holy Spirit;
as in the beginning, so now and for ever. Amen.**

...

Be exalted O God, above the heavens
And your glory be over all the earth.
Your loving-kindness is higher than the heavens
Your faithfulness reaches to the clouds.

*...expressions of praise and thanks may be made
silently or aloud ...*

Our God in heaven, father and mother to us,
Hope of the nations, Fulfilment of the desires of the
ages

Hallowed be your name!

Concerns and biddings for the good of the world and God's desires may be mentioned here or after each or all of the following petitions.

In a world needing wisdom to read its own stars, faithful God,
glorify your name.
Among those who are excluded and held at the margins, faithful God,
glorify your name.
In the search for meaning and fullness of life, faithful God,
glorify your name.
In the naming and framing of new knowledge, faithful God,
glorify your name.

...other petitions may be made...

In pursuit of God's just and gentle ways, we find ourselves in need of means and sustenance

Pause to recognise our needs

As you provide for us, sustain us and equip us to serve you, faithful God,
glorify your name.

Yet our ways have too often not pursued God's agenda and have got in the way of God's priorities.

... Pause to bring our wrongs repentantly to God...

As we turn from our sins and turn to Christ this day faithful God,

glorify your name.

And we have failed to extend to others the courtesy
of the forgiveness and forbearance we ourselves
enjoy and rely upon.

> *... we recall before God our sense of being*
> *wronged and release forgiveness ..*

As we forgo our claims on others for revenge. and
recompense for wrongs
faithful God,
glorify your name.

As we seek to be guided by the star of Christ's
coming and be faithful to our baptism, let us reflect
on what challenges to our faithfulness and integrity
the coming hours may bring, and pause respectfully
before the many unknowns of our future.

> *Pause for recollection ....*

Today into our lives we weave
The ways of God with the air we breathe.
Facing times of trial and stress
We call upon God's power to bless.
When we pass through joyful things
We make to God our thanksgivings.
All who in body or mind we meet
May God through us both touch and greet.
In every task and deed that's done
We weave the purpose of the Son.

Friday

On Fridays, many of the prayers reflect the theme of the passion and crucifixion of Christ.

As the deer pants for streams of water, so my soul longs after you, O God.
My soul thirsts for you, the living God.

...

What is it that we seek?
We seek God's reign and righteousness.
Let's seek with all our reflecting
Amen. God be our wisdom.
Let's seek with all our attentiveness
Amen. God be our centre
Let's seek with all our valuing
Amen. God be our vision.
Let's seek with all our efforts
Amen. God be our souls' shelter

...

On the cross, Jesus framed fracturing-life's ebb with words from scripture,
May we frame our lives' flow primed by God's word.
Let us attend!

> *Collects, Psalm(s) and readings. There may be a time of quiet and/or shared reflection. A framework for reflection, (p.139) may be used.*

Jesus call us to faith in Him.

> *pause for reflection*

Lord, we believe,
help us in our unbelief.

Though in the form of God,
Christ did not regard equality with God
as something to be held.
He emptied himself,
taking on the form of a slave.
Jesus was born in human likeness;
and found in human form.
He humbled himself
and was obedient into death—
even death on a cross.
Therefore God highly exalted Christ
giving the name above every name.
So at the name of Jesus
every knee should bow,
in heaven and on earth and under the earth,
and every tongue confess
that Jesus Christ is Lord,
to the glory of God the Father.

From Philippians 2

...

We will give God thanks:
You are our help and our God.

Blessèd and hallowed is your name, compassionate,
gracious and merciful God, you seek us out in the
darkness of our sin, you exchange beauty of
reconciliation for the ashes of our rebellion as you
come to us with healing in your wings.

Father in heaven
Hallowed be your name.

We have been led into a world seemingly deserted of meaning, we pray for those who hunger and thirst for righteousness, that they may be filled

...

Your kingdom come, your will be done:
Let us live by the word that comes from your mouth.

...

In a world of insecurity and danger, we pray for the protection of the vulnerable

...

Your kingdom come, your will be done:
Let us live by the word that comes from your mouth.
In a world of powers and ambition, we pray for those who make decisions affecting the lives of others

...

Your kingdom come, your will be done:
Let us live by the word that comes from your mouth.
In a world needing the ministry of angels in many guises, some unawares, we pray for the needs and concerns known to us.

...

Your kingdom come, your will be done:
Let us live by the word that comes from your mouth.

In a world where there is bread enough for all, we
bring before you those who do not have and pray for
the will and means of supply, globally and locally

...

Your kingdom come, your will be done:
**Let us live by the word that comes from your
mouth**
seeking first your kingdom & righteousness, may all
things needful be added to us.

Prayers for needs may be voiced....

You open your hand and satisfy the desires of every
living thing.

...

Search me, O God, and know my heart;
test me and know my thoughts.
See if there is any wicked way in me,
and lead me in the way everlasting
Ps.139:23-4

Have mercy on us, O God,
according to your steadfast love
wash us thoroughly from our iniquity,
and cleanse us from our sin.
Create in us a clean heart, O God,
and renew a right spirit within us.
Do not take your holy spirit from us
Restore to us the joy of your salvation
See. Ps.51

O Soul be joyful; the loving God stretches out his
merciful hand to you.

...

Make us instruments of your peace:
and let your glory be over all the earth.

...pause to reflect on the coming day...

Tempted to breaden stones:
May your Word give us life.
Tested by intimations of invincibility:
Make us wise in your ways.
Trialled by the seductions of power:
Keep us true to you.

Saturday

Saturday's prayers tend to reflect the theme of the Kingdom season: Christ's light being brought to the darkness of world and life into death

You are the fountain of life;
in your light we see light.
Your word is a lantern to our feet
and a light upon our paths.
Sustain us according to your promise
and we shall live.
My soul faints with longing for your salvation,
and in your word have I put my hope.

Psalm 35:9; 119:105, 116, 147

Collects, Psalm(s) and readings.

The word be that goes out from God's mouth shall not return empty,
it shall accomplish God's purpose,
and succeed in what it is sent to do.

Isaiah 55:11

Quiet and/or shared reflection. A framework for reflection, (p.139) may be used.

...

The following Canticle may be said or some other.

Great and wonderful are your deeds,
Lord God the Almighty.
Just and true are your ways,
O ruler of the nations.
Who shall not revere and praise your name,
O Lord?

For you alone are holy.
All nations shall come and worship in your
presence:
for your just dealings have been revealed.
To the One who sits on the throne
and to the Lamb
be blessing and honour
glory and might,
for ever and ever. Amen.

Adapted from text © The
Archbishops' Council of the
Church of England

...

O Lord, open our lips
And our mouth shall proclaim your praise.
Blessèd are you, Heaven's High King and judge of
all, we give you praise and honour for with you is the
well of life,
In your light we see light.

Praise and thanksgiving, silent or aloud.

God in heaven; father and mother to us,
Hallowed be your name
Your will is for the Light of Christ to illumine
everyone. May your light shine on all for whom we
pray and chase the shadows from the situations we
are concerned about.

We bring our concerns for people or events to
God, silently or aloud.

In the kingdom of light, death will be no more;
mourning and crying and pain will be no more and
God will wipe away every tear.

...

Faithful One, chase the shadows from this age, ripen
the first fruits of your will on earth:
Your kingdom come.

In that day, of the increase of Christ's government
and of peace there shall be no end.

...

Faithful One, chase the shadows from this age, ripen
the first fruits of your will on earth:
Your kingdom come.

In that day, your Spirit will fill all things and all shall
know you.

...

Faithful One, chase the shadows from this age, ripen
the first fruits of your will on earth:
Your kingdom come.

As we seek to walk in Light, you promise to supply
our need

sharing of needs, silently or aloud ....

Seeking first your righteousness
All things shall be added.

Jesus proclaimed 'The Kingdom of God is at hand,
change your outlook and commit yourselves to the
Good News'

*We pause to recognise what of our life needs to
change in the light of God's priorities.*

When the shadows we have cast have hidden the light for others,
Father forgive.

We reflect on what we may need to forgive

We forgive the shadows others have cast on our lives.
Father forgive.

...

This we call to mind and therefore we have hope:
The steadfast love of the love never ceases,
God's mercies never come to an end:
They are new every morning,
Great is your faithfulness, O Lord:
great is your faithfulness.

Lamentations 3:19 ff

We reflect on the coming day: its potential challenges to our living out the Good News and recognising it may bring things for which we are unprepared.

...

In all that today may bring; the anticipated and the surprising; the pleasant and the testing; go before us, alert us to the real issues,

strengthen us for Good,
awaken us if we sleepwalk into sin,
show us the way out of the Darkness
and fill us with love, hope and peace
as we cling fast to you.
Amen.

Everyday Prayer

This is an option for use on any day. It could be used as a change from other daily offices or If you wish to say two offices in a day, this could be one and a named-day office or seasonal one the other.

Seek while the Lord may be found,
call out while God is near;
let the wicked forsake their way,
and the unrighteous their thoughts.

> *Pause to acknowledge God's presence.*

We do not live by bread alone
but by every word that comes from the mouth of God.

> *Collect, Psalm(s) and readings.*

God's word is very near to us;
it is in our mouths and in our hearts for us to observe.

> *There may be a time of quiet and/or shared reflection. A framework for reflection(p.139) may be used.*

> *The following Canticle may be said or some other*

O God, Your thoughts are not our thoughts,
nor are our ways your ways, O Lord.
For as the heavens are higher than the earth,
so are your ways higher than our ways
and your thoughts than our thoughts.
For as the rain and the snow come down from heaven,

and do not return there until they have watered the earth,
making it bring forth and sprout,
giving seed to the sower and bread to the eater,
so shall your word be that goes out from your mouth;
it shall not return to you empty,
but it shall accomplish what you purpose,
and succeed in what you sent it for.
For we shall go out in joy, and be led back in peace;
the mountains and the hills shall burst into song,
and all the trees of the field shall clap their hands.

see Isaiah 55.8-12

O Lord open our lips:
and our mouth shall proclaim your praise

Blessed are you merciful and gracious God, you are slow to anger, and abound in steadfast love and faithfulness, you are full of compassion and forgiveness.

Hallowed be your name!

> *Songs and/or extempore prayers of praise and thanks ...*

The hallowing of your name echo through the universe!
Gracious God, may your will be done:
on earth as in heaven.

Let us catch glimpses of heaven today; inspire us to sense how your will may be transfused into our world's life, as we pray now.

Concerns for the good of people and events are brought before God, silently or aloud …

Compassionate God, may your will be done:
on earth as in heaven.

We seek your kingdom and righteousness, give all things needful to us in our seeking

… sharing of needs in silence or aloud…

In our asking for your provision, Generous God, may your will be done:
on earth as in heaven.

Give us today the resolve to forgive others: as you forgive us …

… quiet reflection on our own admissions of wrong and on forgiving …

forgiven and forgiving;
Merciful God, may your will be done:
on earth as in heaven.

Faithful One, be with us in the challenges to our faith and integrity: do not let us fall away from you…

… we consider the coming day…

Guide us O God:
by your light to live
by your grace, forgive
to speak well to all

to act on your call
in storm find your rest
in others, seek their best
Your wisdom to know
Christ's presence to show
Father, may we be, in this world, the leaven
And may your will be done on earth
as it is in heaven.

Everyday Prayer -form 2

This everday order of service uses texts almost exclusively drawn from Paul's letters. These phrases and passages are edited to be used as prayers.

What was written in the Scriptures long ago was for our learning; to give us hope and encouragement as we wait patiently for the fulfilment of God's promises.

Collects, Psalm(s) and readings.

We have heard the Holy Scriptures, They are able to make us wise for salvation
through faith in Christ Jesus.

Reflection (together with others where possible), silently and/or aloud. A framework for reflection, (p.139) may be used.

All Scripture is God-breathed and is useful for teaching, rebuking, correcting and training in righteousness,
so that the servant of God may be equipped for every good work

2 Timothy 3:16

After the readings and reflection, the following Canticle may be said or some other.

Jesus Christ is the image of the invisible God, the firstborn over all creation.
For in Christ all things were created:
things in heaven and on earth, visible and invisible,
whether thrones or powers
or rulers or authorities;

**all things have been created
through him and for him.
He is before all things,
and in him all things hold together.
And he is the head of the body, the church;
he is the beginning
and the firstborn from among the dead,
so that in everything
he might have the supremacy.
For God was pleased
to have all his fullness dwell in him,
and through him to reconcile to himself
all things,
whether things on earth or things in heaven,
by making peace through his blood,
shed on the cross.**

From Colossians 1:16ff

Hallowed be your name Father Through the Son in the Holy Spirit,

As in the beginning so now and forever. Amen.

We did not receive a spirit that makes us slaves to fear

We received the Spirit of adoption.

Your Spirit testifies with ours that we are your children:

By your Spirit we cry "Abba! Father"

Praise be to you, God and Father of our Lord Jesus Christ, Father of compassion and God of all comfort. We give thanks to you at all times and for everything **in the name of our Lord Jesus Christ.**

...

Nothing in all creation, will be able to separate us
from your love, O God, in Christ Jesus our Lord.

Blessed are you God
Hallowed be your name.

Help us and all your church to bear with one another
in love, making every effort to maintain the unity of
the Spirit in the bond of peace, we pray for all
humility and gentleness, with patience.

...

We bow our knees before you, Father, and your
Spirit intercedes in our weakness;
for we do not know how to pray as we ought.

We pray that when your witnesses throughout the
world speak, a message may be given to make
known with boldness the mystery of the gospel

...

We bow our knees before you, Father, and your
Spirit intercedes in our weakness;
for we do not know how to pray as we ought.

We remember those in hardship, or distress, or
persecution, or famine, or nakedness, or peril, or
sword.

...

We bow our knees before you, Father, and your
Spirit intercedes in our weakness;
for we do not know how to pray as we ought.

We eagerly anticipate that the creation itself will be
set free from its bondage to decay and will obtain the

freedom of the glory of the children of God. We pray for the whole creation, groaning in labour pains until now;

     ...

We bow our knees before you, Father, and your Spirit intercedes in our weakness;
for we do not know how to pray as we ought.

*   other concerns, voiced or silently prayed ...*

We bow our knees before you, Father, and your Spirit intercedes in our weakness;
for we do not know how to pray as we ought.

You supply seed to the sower and bread for food, supply and multiply our seed for sowing and increase the harvest of our righteousness.

     ...

We bow our knees before you, Father, and your Spirit intercedes in our weakness;
for we do not know how to pray as we ought.

just as the Lord has forgiven us, so we also must forgive.

     ...

There is therefore now no condemnation for those who are in Christ Jesus.
Thanks be to God

Strengthen our hearts in holiness that we may be blameless before you Father God at the coming of our Lord Jesus with all his saints.

     ...

Now to you who by the power at work within us are able to accomplish abundantly far more than all we can ask or imagine, to you be glory in the church and in Christ Jesus
to all generations, forever and ever. Amen.

Seasons, festivals and special days.

There are times in the year when for varying amounts of time, the church has celebrated particular events, people and sometimes doctrines. The liturgical year is generally accounted as starting in Advent, and so the order of offices in this section also starts there and moves round the year in sequence from there. This selection here offers some suggestions for change, such as for a longer Advent and also some seasons that are just becoming accepted (Creationtide) or which might simply be a nice idea and offer some variation (Transfiguration).

For those less familiar with the liturgical year and to help introduce the extra days and seasons offered in this book, here is a quick guide to the seasons and days in the order they are set out and with some guidance as to when they take place. There is a fuller description given for each in the introductory remarks to each under their headings.

Advent takes place in the run up to Christmas. In the past few hundred years in the West it has started on the fourth Sunday before Christmas (very often the first Sunday of December) and goes on until the evening before Christmas day. In the East it starts in mid November.

Christmas starts on the eve of 25 December and goes on till 5 January -the Twelve Days of Christmas.

Epiphany Starts on 6 January and generally goes on until The Feast of the Presentation of Christ in the Temple -traditionally known as 'Candlemas' which takes place on 2 February.

Presentation or 'Candlemas' is 2 February and marks a kind of mid-point between Christmas and Lent.

Lent is dependent on the date of Easter which varies because it is based on a lunar calendar, but in any case is the next major season, it's just that its start date varies.

Passiontide and Holy Week start two Sundays and one Sunday before Easter day respectively. The mark a fuller focus on the Crucifixion and the suffering of Christ.

Eastertide starts on the eve of Easter day and last for seven weeks.

Ascensiontide starts the Thursday ten days before Pentecost Sunday.

Pentecost season starts 50 days after Easter day.
'

Magnificat days and seasons -this is a way of holding together a varied collection of remembrances of the Virgin Mary which occur at various times of the year: Candlemas is often considered one, Annunciation on 25 March, the Visitation of Mary to Elizabeth on 31 May, are two with Biblical foundation and there are also 15 August and 8 September for her death and birth respectively.

Transfiguration is on 8 August and is considered fairly major in the Eastern churches.

Creationtide is a new season in the West starting at the beginning of September and ending with the feast of St Francis of Assissi on 4 October.

Kingdom Season is during November and ends with Advent Sunday.

Dark Seasons is simply an alternative form of prayer using themes of light and darkness with use during the times of the year in northern latitudes when the nights are long.

A Pauline Order is not really a season (though it could be used on 25 January when St Paul is commemorated) but an alternative form of prayer using phrases and imagery from the letters of Paul.

Advent -the run up to Christmas

Advent traditionally begins the Church's year and starts on the fourth Sunday before Christmas. However, the timing of Advent has varied through Church history and still does (in the Orthodox East it is 40 days, like Lent, beginning in the middle of November). So it may be good to think about using this form of prayer from mid-November and perhaps be open to moving onto the Christmas form a few days before Christmas day if this better suits your personal context. This season majors on the themes of Christ's return and the consummation of creation at the End of all things.

We hope for your salvation, O Lord,
and all our ways are before you.
The unfolding of your words gives light;
it imparts understanding to the simple.
We long for your salvation, O God,
and your lore[2] is our delight.

See Psalm119

Pause to recognise God's presence.

My soul faints with longing for your salvation,
and in your word have I put my hope.

Collect, Psalm and readings...

The word that goes out from God's mouth
shall not return empty,
it shall accomplish God's purpose,
and succeed in what it is sent to do.

Isaiah 55:11

Quiet and/or shared reflection. A framework for reflection, (p.139) may be used...

The following Canticle may be said or some other

Blessed are you, Lord God of Israel;
you have come to your people and set us free.
You have raised up for us a mighty Saviour,
born of the house of your servant David.
Through your holy prophets you promised of old
to save us from our enemies,

from the hands of all who hate us;
to show mercy to our forebears
and to remember your holy covenant.
This was the oath you swore to our father
Abraham:
to set us free from the hands of our enemies,
free to worship you without fear,
holy and righteous before you,
all the days of our life.
In your tender compassion, O God
the dawn from on high shall break upon us,
to shine on those who dwell in darkness and the
shadow of death,
and to guide our feet into the way of peace.

Based on the ELLC version of the
Benedictus

O Lord, open our lips
And our mouth shall proclaim your praise.
We have waited on your loving-kindness, O God,
in the midst of your temple.
As with your name, O God,
so your praise reaches to the ends of the earth;
your right hand is full of justice.
Hallowed be your name!

See Psalm 48:9-10

...when any further expressions of praise and
thanks have been shared:

Our God in heaven, father and mother to us:
Hallowed be your name

'See, the home of God is among mortals. He will
dwell with them; they will be his peoples, and God
himself will be with them; he will wipe every tear

from their eyes. Death will be no more; mourning and crying and pain will be no more, for the first things have passed away.'

Revelation 21.3-4

Bring in your Reign, O God;
Let your vision prevail.

A day is coming and has already come when all good hopes will blossom and wickedness will die back never to be remembered. Just and merciful God, hasten that Day and in this age give us a foretaste of your kingdom.

Bring in your Reign, O God;
Let your vision prevail.

> *Concerns and biddings for the good of the world and God's desires may be mentioned here or after each or all of the following petitions*

In that day, death and mourning, crying and pain will be no more and God will wipe away every tear.

Bring in your Reign, O God;
Let your vision prevail.

In that Day, of the increase of Christ's government and peace there shall be no end.

Bring in your Reign, O God;
Let your vision prevail.

In that Day, your Spirit will fill all things and all shall know you.

Bring in your Reign, O God;

Let your vision prevail.

As we walk the path of your Dream of a healed creation, may we know your hand supplying our needs.
> *... recalling of needs in silence or aloud*

As we ask for daily bread.

Bring in your Reign, O God;
Let your vision prevail.

Give us this day the courage and insight to forgive others as you forgive us our trespasses.

> *... a moment of silence for recollection and response to this call ...*

in our forgiving and being forgiven,
Bring in your Reign, O God;
Let your vision prevail.

As we seek to forge a new future living the new life of Christ, let us reflect on what challenges to our faithfulness and integrity the coming hours may bring, and pause before the many unknowns of our future

> *...*

When we are tested by temptation
strengthen us.
When our commitment to your Love is put to trial,
save us.
When evil ensnares
free us.
For yours is the kingdom, the power and the glory,

now and forever. Amen
Amen! Blessing and glory and wisdom
and thanksgiving and honour
and power and might
be to our God for ever and ever!   **Amen!**
from Revelation 7:12

Christmas

Christmas prayers reflect the theme of God becoming human. Traditionally, in the West, Christmas starts after sundown on 24 December and lasts until 5 January (Twelfth Night) and the season of Epiphany begins on 6 January. However, there is a mismatch now between wider secular society and the Church's year. In wider society Christmas seems to end or at least come to a climax on 25 December. So it may feel helpful to start to pray the Christmas office earlier in December and finish a day or three after 25th.

O God open our souls
to awaken to your presence
O God open our minds
to hear your call
O God open our hearts
to know your love
O God open our lives
to be fully alive in you and to our neighbour.

...

As we hear the scriptures read, may they lead us to the Christ and may we find in Jesus the fulfilment of all our searching.

> *Collects, Psalm(s) and readings. There may be a time of quiet and/or shared reflection. A framework for reflection (see p.139), using the pattern of the Lord's prayer may be used.*

Blessed are those who hear the word of God
And obey it.

> *The following Canticle may be said or some other*

My soul proclaims your greatness O Lord;
my spirit rejoices in you O God our Saviour,
You have looked with favour on your lowly
servant.
From this day all generations will call us
blessed:
Almighty, you have done great things for us,
and holy is your name.
You have mercy on those who fear you
from generation to generation.
You have shown strength with your arm
and scattered the proud in their conceit,
casting down the mighty from their thrones
and lifting up the lowly.
you have filled the hungry with good things,
and sent the rich away empty.
You have come to the help of your servant Israel,
remembering your promise of mercy,
the promise made to our forebears,
to Abraham and his children forever.

Based on the ELLC version of
Luke 1:46-55

...

Glory to God in the highest:
and on earth -peace and goodwill.
Lord God, heavenly King,
almighty God and Father,
we worship you, we give you thanks,
we praise you for your glory.

...expressions of of praise and thanks ...

O God, you have done great things for us

And holy is your name.

...

Your heavenly will be done in all created beings!
May your commonwealth of peace and freedom
sustain our hope and come on earth.
Father, may your will be fleshed out:
on earth as in heaven.

.....

Your will is for the liberation of creation in bondage
to decay
Father, may your will be be fleshed out:
on earth as in heaven.
Your will is for peace and justice,
Father, may your will be be fleshed out:
on earth as in heaven.
Your will is for all to come to a knowledge of
salvation
Father, may your will be fleshed out:
on earth as in heaven.

> *Concerns and biddings for the good of the world
> and God's desires might be mentioned here.*

With the bread we need for today, feed us.
Into what will sustain our life in you, lead us.

> *... reflection and requests for daily bread and
> provision.*

We look to you to supply our need.
Be our provider and strength.
Father, may your will be be fleshed out:
on earth as in heaven.

Forgiving God, we have held onto your gifts and stayed aloof.

...

God forgive us
And Let grace live within us

Sharing God; we have resisted your life within us.

...

God forgive us
And Let grace live within us

...

God who first loved us, help us to love others by forgiving

....

God forgive us
And Let grace live within us

> *There may be silence to reflect on forgiving. After an appropriate interval, words of forgiveness may be said.*

As we seek to live embodying the values and commitments of God's just and gentle Rule, let us reflect on likely forthcoming challenges to our faithfulness and integrity, and let's recognise our future has many unknowns to wrongfoot us.

...

We are called to bear Christ into our world. With Mary we ask, how can this be?

> *Pause for reflection.*

We take to heart the Angel's reply:

The power of the Most High will overshadow you;
with God it is possible:
Let it be to us according to your Word.

Epiphany

The season of Epiphany starts on 6 January and ends on 1 February. It highlights Christ's revelation to the world and fulfilment of the desires of the ages. The biblical themes recalled are the visit of the Magi, Christ's Baptism and the first miracle ie changing of water into wine.

Let us pray that the flame of God's loving presence may spring up in our hearts and transform us by the knowledge of divine glory.

> ...
> *A light or lights may be lit as the following prayer is said by all:*

We take refuge in the Divine Light,
The Flame of Truth
The soul's Ray
We take refuge in the Embodiment of Glory
The Lamp of our path
The Essence of love

> *Based on a prayer from the*
> *Church of South India*

As we hear the scriptures read, may they lead us to the Christ, and may we find in Jesus the fulfilment of all our searching.

> *Collect, Psalm and readings.*

Blessed are those who hear the word of God
And do it.

> *Quiet and/or shared reflection. A framework for reflection, (p.139) may be used.*

At Jesus's baptism, a voice from heaven said, 'This is my Son, the Beloved, with whom I am well pleased.'
We see and testify that this is the Son of God.

See Matthew 3:17 & John 1:34

The following Canticle may be said or some other

Now, Lord, you let your servant go in peace:
your word has been fulfilled.
My own eyes have seen the salvation
which you have prepared in the sight of every
people:
a light to reveal you to the nations
and the glory of your people Israel.

ELLC translation of Luke 2:29-32

Hallowed be your name, Father, through the Son
in the Holy Spirit;
as in the beginning, so now and for ever. Amen.

...

Be exalted O God, above the heavens
And your glory be over all the earth.
Your loving-kindness is higher than the heavens
Your faithfulness reaches to the clouds.

...expressions of praise and thanks may be made silently or aloud ...

Our God in heaven, father and mother to us, Hope of the nations, Fulfilment of the desires of the ages
Hallowed be your name

Concerns and biddings for the good of the world and God's desires may be mentioned here or after the following petitions.

In a world needing wisdom to read its own stars, faithful God,
glorify your name.
Among those who are excluded and held at the margins, faithful God,
glorify your name.
In the search for meaning and fullness of life, faithful God,
glorify your name.
In the naming and framing of new knowledge, faithful God,
glorify your name.

…other petitions may be made…

In pursuit of God's just and gentle ways, we find ourselves in need of means and sustenance

Pause to recognise our needs

As you provide for us, sustain us and equip us to serve you, faithful God,
glorify your name.

...

We turn again to recognise that our ways have too often not followed God's agenda and we have strayed from God's priorities.

…. Pause to bring our wrongs repentantly to God…

As we turn from our sins and turn to Christ this day, faithful God,
glorify your name.

We have failed to extend to others the courtesy of the forgiveness and forbearance we ourselves enjoy and rely upon.

> *... we recall before God our sense of being wronged and release forgiveness ...*

As we forgo our claims on others for revenge and recompense for wrongs, faithful God,
glorify your name.

> ...

As we seek to be guided by the star of Christ's coming and to be faithful to our baptism, let us reflect on what challenges to our faithfulness and integrity the coming hours may bring, and pause respectfully before the many unknowns of our future.

> *Pause for recollection...*

Today into our lives we weave
The ways of God with the air we breathe.
Facing times of trial and stress
we call upon God's power to bless.
When we pass through joyful things
we make to God our thanksgivings.
All who in body or mind we meet
may God through us both touch and greet.
In every task and deed that's done
we weave the purpose of the Son.

Presentation of Christ also known as Candlemas

The Presentation of Christ in the Temple recalls Jesus being taken to the Temple by his parents forty days after his birth. So it is counted from Christmas day and gives a date of 2 February.

We bring ourselves here and present ourselves to God:
the Lord whom we seek comes to his temple.
The true light that lightens all has come into the world,
In your light may we see light.
Leading us, from delusion to truth,
and into your righteous way.
Lead us, Source of all Being, Father and Mother to us:
From darkness to light and into your gracious will.
Lead us, Christ, our Friend and our Brother;
From death to eternal life and into your infinite joy;
Lead us, Divine Spirit, empowering Life within
for we seek your enabling touch.

*Based on a prayer from the
Church of South India*

As we hear the scriptures read, let us be transformed by the renewing of our minds, to discern the will of God -what is good and acceptable and perfect.

Drawn from Romans 12:2

As we reflect, Holy Spirit, rest upon us.

Nourished in what is revealed by the Holy Spirit
May we grow and became strong in faith,
filled with wisdom;
And with the favour of God upon us

The following Canticle, or some other

**Now, Lord, you let your servant go in peace:
your word has been fulfilled.
My own eyes have seen the salvation
which you have prepared in the sight of every
people;
A light to reveal you to the nations
and the glory of your people Israel.**

*English translation of the Nunc Dimittis, Luke
2:29-32, copyright © 1988, by the English
Language Liturgical Consultation. Used
within terms of licence*

Glory to God in the highest:
and on earth -peace and goodwill.
Lord God, heavenly King,
almighty God and Father,
we worship you, we give you thanks,
we praise you for your glory.

...expressions of of praise and thanks ...

Our God in heaven, father and mother to us, Light of
the nations, Fulfilment of the desires of the ages.
Hallowed be your name
In a world needing revelation to lighten our
darkness,
faithful God,
glorify your name.
Among those who await consolation and
redemption,
faithful God,
glorify your name.
In the search for meaning and fullness of life,
faithful God,
glorify your name.
Among those who bring good to workers, widows,
and among those who show mercy to migrants.
faithful God,
glorify your name.
> *...other petitions may be made, each ending with*

faithful God,
glorify your name.
> ...

The company of those who seek your face, O God,
shall receive a blessing from you.
> *[Cf Ps.24]*

With the bread we need for today, feed us.
Into what will sustain our life in you, lead us.

> *Pause to recognise our needs*

As you provide for us, sustain us and equip us to
serve you,
faithful God,

glorify your name.

...

When the shadows we have cast have hidden the
light for others,
Father forgive.
We offer the light of forgiveness for the shadows
others have cast on our lives.
Father forgive.
You are the fountain of life;
in your light we see light.
Your word is a lantern to our feet
and a light upon our paths.

...

Though we walk in the midst of trouble, O God;
you will preserve us.
You will stretch forth your hand against the fury of
our enemies;
your right hand will save us.
Make good your purpose for us;
your loving-kindness, O Lord, endures for ever
forsake not the work of your hands.
Make good your purpose for us.

[Ps. 138:6-8]

Master, now you dismiss your servant in peace,
according to your word;
for my eyes have seen your salvation.

Lent

During Lent we reflect on our need for God's grace and mercy and we commit ourselves to growth in holiness and wisdom.

Remembering we are dust and to dust we shall return, we turn from our waywardness to cultivate Christwardness.

What is it that we seek?
We seek God's way in the wilderness.
Let's seek with all our deciding
Amen. God be our wisdom.
Let's seek with all our affections
Amen. God be our centre
Let's seek with all our attitudes
Amen. God be our vision.
Let's seek with all our resources
Amen. God be our mainstay.

...

Tested and tempted in the desert, scripture revealed and steered Jesus' resistance and direction. May we learn and inwardly digest the Wisdom of God we hear.

Let us attend!

> *Collects, Psalm(s) and readings.. There may be a time of quiet and/or shared reflection. A framework for reflection (p.139), using the pattern of the Lord's prayer may be used ...*

Jesus call us to faith in Him.

....pause for reflection

Lord, we believe,
help us in our unbelief.

The following Canticle may be said or some other

Though in the form of God,
Christ did not regard equality with God
as something to be held.
He emptied himself,
taking on the form of a slave.
Jesus was born in human likeness;
and found in human form.
He humbled himself
and was obedient into death—
even death on a cross.
Therefore God highly exalted him
giving him the name above every name.
So at the name of Jesus
every knee should bow,
in heaven and on earth and under the earth,
and every tongue confess
that Jesus Christ is Lord,
to the glory of God the Father.

From Philippians 2

...

We will give God thanks:
You are our help and our God.

You are gracious and compassionate, slow to anger
and abounding in steadfast faithful love. You seek
us out in the darkness of our sin, and exchange

beauty of reconciliation for the ashes of our rebellion.

...other appreciations of God may be added.

Our God in heaven, father and mother to us;
Hallowed be your name.

...

We have been led into deserts of dried-up meaning and conflicting desires. We petition for those who hunger and thirst for righteousness, that they may be filled

God fulfil your purpose for us:
Send from heaven and save us.

We find ourselves in a world of precarity and danger, we cry out for the vulnerable and marginalised that they may find respite and dignity.

God fulfil your purpose for us:
Send from heaven and save us.

In a world replete with prideful powers and vaunting ambition, we remember before God those who make decisions affecting the lives of others that they may grow in wisdom and compassion.

God fulfil your purpose for us:
Send from heaven and save us.

In a world needing the ministry of angels in many guises, some unawares, we lay out the needs and concerns known to us.

Further concerns may be voiced here.

God fulfil your purpose for us:
Send from heaven and save us.

In a world where there is bread enough for all, we bring before you those who do not have and pray for the will and means of supply, globally and locally

God fulfil your purpose for us:
Send from heaven and save us.

...

Seeking first your kingdom & righteousness may all things needful be added to us.

Prayers for needs may be voiced....

You open your hand
and satisfy the desires of every living thing.

We recognise ourselves in the fractured and frail failures of the stories of God's people. and we pause to reorient ourselves towards love of God and neighbour.

Love is patient; love is kind; love is not envious or boastful or arrogant or rude.

Our love has been as the morning mist, as the dew that goes early away.
God be gracious;
Lord, have mercy

Love does not insist on its own way; it is not irritable or resentful; Love does not rejoice in wrongdoing, but rejoices in the truth

Our love has been as the morning mist, as the dew
that goes early away.
God be gracious;
Lord, have mercy

Love bears all things, believes all things, hopes all
things, endures all things.

Our love has been as the morning mist, as the dew
that goes early away.
God be gracious;
Lord, have mercy

Cf. 1 Cor 13:4-7; Hosea 13:3

O Soul be joyful; our merciful God stretches out a
loving hand to you.

    ...

Make us instruments of your peace:
and let your glory be over all the earth.

    ...pause to reflect on the coming day...

Tempted to breaden stones:
May your Word give us life.
Tested by intimations of invincibility:
Make us wise in your ways.
Trialled by the seductions of power:
Keep us true to you.

Passiontide and Holy Week

*Passiontide begins on the Sunday before Palm Sunday
and takes us up to Easter Sunday. The focus is on the
passion and crucifixion of Christ. During this time our
prayers reflect the suffering and death of Christ.*

Our hearts tell of your Word, O God, "Seek my face".
Your face, Lord, will we seek
Ps.27

What is it that we seek?
We seek God's heart and holiness.
Let's seek with all our reflecting
Amen. God be our wisdom.
Let's seek with all our attentiveness
Amen. God be our centre.
Let's seek with all our valuing
Amen. God be our vision.
Let's seek with all our efforts
Amen. God be our strength and refuge.

...

On the cross, Jesus framed fracturing-life's ebb with
words from scripture,
may we frame our lives' flow primed by God's lore.
Let us attend!

> *Collects, Psalm(s) and readings.. There may be a
> time of quiet and/or shared reflection (p.139).
> using the pattern of the Lord's prayer may be
> used.*

Jesus call us to take up our cross and follow him.

> *…. pause for consideration*

Lord, we believe,
help us in our unbelief.

The following Canticle or some other

The message of the cross
is foolishness to those who are perishing,
but to us who are being saved
it is the power of God.
For since, in the wisdom of God,
the world did not know God through wisdom,
God decided, through the foolishness of our
proclamation,
to save those who believe.
For some demand signs and others desire
wisdom,
but we proclaim Christ crucified,
a stumbling-block to some and foolishness to
others.
But to those who are the called,
Christ is the power of God and the wisdom of
God.
For God's foolishness is wiser than human
wisdom,
and God's weakness is stronger than human
strength.

From 1 Corinthians 1:18-25

...

O God, you so loved us, that you gave your only
begotten so that we might not perish but have
eternal life:

long-suffering God, slow to anger, unlimited in grace
and infinite in mercy, for the joy you set before him,

Jesus endured; endured betrayal, crowd-pleasing,
the little collusions and small infidelities that set you
at cross purposes to the system,

Father in heaven
Hallowed be your name.

Thanks and praise may be shared…

As we dare to intercede for a breaking world, we fear
that our human agendas and earth-framed ideas fall
short of true wisdom. So we ask not for our will but
yours to be done.

For the misled and the disregarded
Not our will
but your will be done.
For the elites and powerful,
Not our will
but your will be done.
For the exploiters of others,
Not our will
but your will be done.
For the fearful and weak,
Not our will
but your will be done.
For the cynical and world-weary,
Not our will
but your will be done.
For the blindly pious and the users of religion,
Not our will
but your will be done.
For those just doing their jobs,
Not our will

but your will be done.
For the helpless and the hopeless,
Not our will
but your will be done.
For the despairing and crushed in spirit
Not our will
but your will be done.

and we ask in hope that our prayerful imaginings
may grow into God's, as we consider the forces in
our times still arrayed for woe and for ill.

Your Kingdom come,
Your will be done on earth as in heaven.

There is bread enough to be broken for all to share
though our sharing is flawed and misdirected, we
ask that all may be the haves, and none the have-
nots.

Your kingdom come, your will be done:
Give us each day our morrowly bread.

Prayers for needs may be voiced….

Seeking first your kingdom & righteousness
May all things needful be added to us.

...

Search me, O God, and know my heart;
test me and know my thoughts.
See if there is any wicked way in me,
and lead me in the way everlasting
Ps.139:23-4

...

We confess with sorrow that we have collaborated
with the fallen powers of this world knowingly or
unwittingly deliberately or from fearful weakness.

We are mortified.
We repent in dust and ashes.
We turn afresh to the way of Christ,
the way of the cross
the way of life-giving wisdom.
Heal us and we shall be healed.
Save us and we shall be saved.
We hear with hope Jesus' words: 'Forgive them'.

...

Make us instruments of your peace:
and let your glory be over all the earth.

...pause to reflect on the coming day...

Tempted to resign ourselves to the way of the world:
Give us fresh vision and graciousness.
Pressured towards unwise compromise:
Strengthen our resolve.
Trialled by the grind of human frailties:
Teach us to remember our own.

Eastertide

Eastertide lasts until Ascensiontide, that is until the celebration of Christ's Ascension, ten days before Pentecost. The prayers for this time reflect Christ's rising from death and its implications.

Alleluia, Christ is risen!
He is risen indeed! Alleluia!
Our hopes are raised
Life emerges from death
Right is wrested from wrong
The uprising of Love has begun!

...

Draw alongside us, Lord Jesus,
Open up the scriptures to us by your Spirit,
so our hearts might be lit with fresh understanding
and fired up by your presence.

> *Collects, Psalm(s) and readings. The reader or service leader, after the readings may say:*

Here ends the reading.
Here begins its outworking.

> *There may be a time of quiet and/or shared reflection. A framework for reflection, (p.139) may be used.*

Jesus said: 'Do not doubt but trust.' With Thomas we respond,
'My Lord and my God!'
Let us hear for ourselves what Jesus replied,
'Blessed are those who have not seen and yet have come to trust.'

...

We have these words so that we may come to
believe and trust:
Jesus is the Messiah, the Son of God,
we have life in his name.

Based on John 20:19ff

The following Canticle may be said or some other

Jesus Christ is the image of the invisible God,
the firstborn over all creation.
For in Christ all things were created:
things in heaven and on earth,
visible and invisible,
whether thrones or powers
or rulers or authorities;
all things have been created
through him and for him.
He is before all things,
and in him all things hold together.
And he is the head of the body, the church;
he is the beginning
and the firstborn from among the dead,
so that in everything
he might have the supremacy.
For God was pleased to have
all his fullness dwell in him,
and through him to reconcile to himself
all things,
whether things on earth or things in heaven,
by making peace through his blood,
shed on the cross.

From Colossians 1:16ff

We set God always before us:
who is at our right hand; we shall not fall.
Our hearts are glad
and our spirits rejoice;
Our flesh shall also rest secure.
For you will not abandon our souls to Death,
nor let your faithful know the Pit.
You will show us the path of life;
in your presence is the fullness of joy
**and in your right hand are pleasures for
evermore**

From Psalm 16

Further appreciation of God may be voiced

O God, roll away the stone from our hearts, and
brighten our imaginations with the dayspring of new
life. In Christ you spoke into the unmaking void of
death, raising your Life from death and enfolding us
in that victory.

God of new creation:
Hallowed be your name

...

We ask for God's eternal-life-giving to be known in
our world, saying:
Living God:
glorify your name

Concerns for the world and its people are brought
before God, either at this point closing with the
series of one-line responses below, or after that
series or using each one-liner to prompt further
prayers.

In our world's global community, in our world's living systems;
Living God:
glorify your name.

In your church as we proclaim your new life in thought and word and deed;

Living God:
glorify your name.

Among all whose lives our lives touch, friends, colleagues and families;

Living God:
glorify your name.

In this world of sin and death, and yet of blessings and common grace;

Living God:
glorify your name.

Rewritten from a prayer in
Patterns of Worship, 1995

...

In our needs and weakness in our provision and supply;
Living God:
glorify your name.

We consider what we need to continue living in Christ

The risen Jesus makes common table with us.
As we make common cause with Christ:
Give us each day our daily bread.

...

Full-lively God, we come to you in sorrow for our sins, and confess to you our weaknesses and unbelief.

Recollection of what we need to confess.

We have fallen back into the law of sin and death, and failed to live the new life of the risen Christ.

Merciful God, forgive us.
And restore us to life.
We have laid others in the tomb of our unforgiveness,
enshrouding them in our contempt and withholding the word of life.
Forgive us, Merciful God
And restore us to life-giving.

Let us attend; Christ breathes upon us the peace and forgiveness of God.

A moment for quiet reflection on our forgiveness.

Who will rescue us from this body of death?
Thanks be to God through Jesus Christ our Lord!

As we seek to forge a new future living the life of Christ let us pause before the likely events and involvements and the unpredictable happenings that face us.
... A collect prayer may be said.

In our laughter, and tears, in our fear and our hope; Living God:

Glorify your name.

...

Jesus comes to us and says,
'Peace be with you. As the Father has sent me, so I send you.'
He breathes on us and says; 'Receive the Holy Spiri.

Pause to reflect on Christ's risen presence and call before we return to the rest of our lives.

Let us bless the Lord:
Thanks be to God
Who gives us the victory
through our Lord Jesus Christ.

Ascensiontide

Ascensiontide is the time between Ascension day and Pentecost Sunday. It recalls Christ's Ascension (see Acts 1) and the theme of waiting on God's Spirit. This order shares some material with the order for Pentecost.

Together with all in Christ, we wait
Come Holy Spirit; soak into our deepest being
We pray together with all your people
Come Holy Spirit; breeze through our staleness.

...

We will hear the scriptures together
Come Holy Spirit; fire up our imaginations for good

...

Glorious Father, give us the Spirit of wisdom and revelation so that we may know you better. Open the eyes of our heart that we may know the hope to which you have called us, the riches of your glorious inheritance and your incomparably great power for us.

From Ephesians 1

Collects, Psalm(s) and readings. are announced and read. When all have been read ...

Reader: God has sent forth the word
May it not return empty.

There may be a time of quiet and/or shared reflection. A framework for reflection (p.139), using the pattern of the Lord's prayer may be used.

Together we say:

**We will receive power
when the Holy Spirit comes upon us;
the same mighty strength
that raised Christ from the dead
and seated him at God's right hand
in the heavenly realms,
far above all rule and authority,
power and dominion,
and every name that is invoked
in the present age and in the one to come.
And we will be Jesus' witnesses
to the ends of the earth**

Acts 1.8 and Ephesians 1.20ff

...

Blessed be the God and Father of our Lord Jesus
Christ,
**You have blessed us in the heavenly realms with
every spiritual blessing in Christ**
to the praise of your glorious grace,
which you have freely given us in the Beloved

*...Prayers and/or songs of praise and thanks may
be shared here...*

And now we give you thanks because In Christ you
take human life to yourself, and do not leave us
orphaned but give gifts by the Holy Spirit, Our God
In heaven, in love you adopted us through Jesus
Christ:
Hallowed be your name!

...

God, send your Spirit: mend your creation, fulfil your promises and inspire your people for good.

Send forth your Spirit:
And renew the face of the earth

May your desires and values spring up and prosper throughout the world, your peace, wholeness and goodness come on earth

Send forth your Spirit:
And renew the face of the earth.

Work righteousness and justice for all the oppressed.

Send forth your Spirit:
And renew the face of the earth.

Through the church, may the manifold wisdom of God be made known to the rulers and authorities in the heavenly realms.

Send forth your Spirit:
And renew the face of the earth.

We ask that all the Lord's holy people have power to grasp how wide and long and high and deep is the love of Christ and be filled to the measure of all the fullness of God

> *…Other prayers or biddings may be voiced here the leader ending with:*

Send forth your Spirit:
And renew the face of the earth.

Let love and faithfulness meet together;
righteousness and peace kiss each other

Send forth your Spirit:
And renew the face of the earth.

...

Be the wind in the sails of our lives and as we are
blown forward by your Spirit may we know your
comfort and provision

> *...prayers or biddings asking for God's provision
> may be added here the leader ending with*

Send forth your Spirit:
And renew the face of our lives.

We have quenched your Spirit in our self-serving or
grudge-bearing

...

Forgive us and renew us:
To know and to offer joyful forgiveness.

...

Blow upon us the breath of life:
And renew the face of our lives.
Make our hearts clean, O God
And reform a right spirit within us.

Let us attend; Christ breathes upon us the peace
and forgiveness of God.

> *A moment for quiet reflection on our forgiveness.*

As we seek to walk in the Spirit let us pause before the likely events and involvements and the unpredictable happenings that face us.

Pause for reflection

Since we live by the Spirit,
let us keep in step with the Spirit.
Gal 5:25

Now to you who by the power at work within us are able to accomplish abundantly far more than all we can ask or imagine, to you be glory in the church and in Christ Jesus to all generations, forever and ever. **Amen**.

Pentecost

During Pentecost (which we might take to be up until Trinity Sunday) we recall first and foremost the gift of the Holy Spirit. Firstly in the coming of the Spirit on the disciples fifty days after Easter -related in Acts 2, and then on the Spirit's presence and action in the Church and the world.

Together with all in Christ, we wait
Come Holy Spirit; soak into our deepest being
We pray together with all your people
Come Holy Spirit; breeze through our staleness.
We will hear the scriptures together
Come Holy Spirit; fire up our imaginations for good
We will rejoin you in the world
Come Holy Spirit; spice us with the savour of Christ

All Scripture is God-breathed and is useful for teaching, rebuking, correcting and training in righteousness,so that we may be equipped for every good work

2 Timothy 3:16

Psalm(s) and readings. are announced and read. When all have been read:

Reader: God has sent forth the word
May it not return empty.

A framework for reflection (p.139), using the pattern of the Lord's prayer may be used.

We affirm our loyalty to God as we say the following Canticle or some other

What we have received
is not the spirit of the world,
but the Spirit who is from God,
so that we may understand
what God has freely given us.
No one can say, "Jesus is Lord,"
except by the Holy Spirit.

1 Corinthians 12:3b

> *Collects may be said. ...*

We did not receive a spirit that makes us slaves to fear
We received the Spirit of adoption
Your Spirit testifies with ours that we are your children:
By your Spirit we cry "Abba! Father"

> *Appreciations of God's goodness and greatness*
> *may be shared...*

Your Spirit hovered over the unformed creation, and overshadowed Mary as the Christ was enwombed, and now your Holy Spirit flares up among us assuring that we are your children, intimating at our core your delight in us,

Our God In heaven, father and mother to us:
Hallowed be your name!

> ...

Creator God, release your Spirit to brood over the desolations of human society; deformed by discordant voices, and damaged by overweaning desires.

Send forth your Spirit:
And renew the face of the earth.

Everliving Lover of our souls, you draw all people to yourself, wooing us Spirit to spirit. We remember before you the work of the gospel as it goes forth not to return empty .

Send forth your Spirit:
And renew the face of the earth.

Passionately faithful God; may the eternal flame of your Spirit burn in our souls and warm the lives of those whose lives we touch in person, process or in prayer.

Send forth your Spirit:
And renew the face of the earth.

Let there be justice, let there be peace and let there be healing

> *...prayers or biddings may be voiced here the leader ending with*

Send forth your Spirit:
And renew the face of the earth.

Be the wind in the sails of our lives and as we are blown forward by your Spirit may we know your comfort and provision

> *...prayers or biddings asking for God's provision may be added here the leader ending with*

Send forth your Spirit:
And renew the face of our worlds.

...

There have been times when we have quenched
your Spirit in our self-serving or grudge-bearing

...

We ask your help so that we might truly repent
and know
and offer
joyful forgiveness,

...

Blow upon us your peace-making breeze:
And renew the face of our lives.
Make our hearts clean, O God
And remake a right spirit within us.

Let us attend; Christ breathes upon us the peace
and forgiveness of God.

A moment for quiet reflection on our forgiveness.

The Spirit of the Lord is on me,
because God has anointed me
to proclaim good news to the poor.
God has sent me to proclaim freedom for the
prisoners
and recovery of sight for the blind,
to set the oppressed free,
to proclaim the year of the Lord's favour.
Luke 4:17-19 and Isaiah 61:1-2

As we seek to walk in the Spirit, let us pause before
the likely events and involvements and the
unpredictable happenings that face us.

...

Since we live by the Spirit,
let us keep in step with the Spirit.

Gal 5:25

Now to you who by the power at work within us are able to accomplish abundantly far more than all we can ask or imagine, to you be glory in the church and in Christ Jesus to all generations, forever and ever. **Amen**.

Ephesians 3:21

Transfiguration

Transfiguration is normally celebrated on 6 August, recalling when Jesus's appearance gloriously changed while on a mountain with some of his disciples. This prayer form might be used for a week or two following that day.

Lord, it is good for us to be here
For your Spirit is with us

> *We pause to recognise God's presence.*

My heart tells of your word, 'Seek my face.'
Your face, Lord, will I seek.
One thing we ask of you Lord
and that alone we seek:
that we may dwell in your house all the days of our life,
To behold your fair beauty and to seek your will.
> *From Ps.27*

> *A song may be sung. Bibles are made ready to be read from.*

As we hear the scriptures
may we listen to your Beloved.
Overshadow us and speak to us
for this comes from the Lord, the Spirit

> *Collects, Psalm(s) and readings. After these have been read:*

Our Lord Jesus Christ received honour and glory from God the Father whose voice was conveyed to him by the Majestic Glory, saying, 'This is my Son, my Beloved, with whom I am well pleased.' By the same Spirit, we hear this voice from heaven, We have the prophetic message more fully confirmed. Let us be attentive to this as to a lamp shining in a dark place.

> *There may be a time of quiet and/or shared reflection. A framework for reflection (p.139), using the pattern of the Lord's prayer may be used.*

> *The following Canticle may be said or some other*

Blessed are you,
O God of our ancestor Israel
for ever and ever.
Yours, O Lord, are the greatness,
the power, the glory,
the victory, and the majesty;
for all that is in the heavens
and on the earth is yours;
yours is the kingdom, O Lord,
and you are exalted as head above all.

1 Chronicles 29:10-11

> *Collect or theme prayers may be said.*

Your steadfast love, O Lord, extends to the heavens,
your faithfulness to the clouds.
Be exalted, O God, above the heavens.
Let your glory be over all the earth.

We honour you and thank you that in Christ we are your beloved children, with whom you are well pleased. In Christ you are transforming us from one degree of glory to another by the working of the Holy Spirit.

[And now we give you thanks because ...]

And so we laud your name:

**Holy, holy, holy God of power and might,
heaven and earth are full of your glory
Hosanna in the highest.**

...

In the stories and hopes of Moses and Elijah, we
glimpse a world transfigured, we ask for
transfigurations of here-and-now realities into
anticipations of the new heaven and new earth.

*Situations of concern may be mentioned. Each
may end with: ...*

Your kingdom come
your will be done on earth as in heaven.

Give us wisdom to share sensitively with all people
the good news so that all may behold your glory in
the face of Jesus Christ. ...

Your kingdom come
your will be done on earth as in heaven.

As we accompany Christ to the wheres and whens
that touch glory, be our provider

...

Your kingdom come
your will be done on earth as in heaven.

...

Forgive us that in various ways, big and small, we have grieved the Spirit as we have resisted being transformed into the likeness of Christ Jesus.

Gracious God, glorify your name,
We glory in your forgiveness.

Enfold our forgiving of others in your transfiguration of creation that we may continually participate in the transformation of the world.

...

Give us grace to forgive:
Work your glory into our forgiveness.
Lead us so we do not sleepwalk into sin
awaken us to the signs of glory around us.
Preserve us from attempts to make permanent the provisional;
And from the paralysing fear of the new and awesome.
In the midst of the strange and misunderstandable;
Give us ears to hear you and heart to follow Jesus.
Yours is the Kingdom, the power and the glory,
now and forever. Amen.
We go being transformed into Christ's image,
from one degree of glory to another;
This comes from the Lord, the Spirit.
Amen.

Creationtide

Creationtide starts on 1 September and goes through to 4 October. It is a time to pray for the sustaining of creation, the protection of vulnerable ecosystems and the promotion of sustainable lifestyles. It is a time to appreciate afresh the beauty and wonder of what God has made.

By wisdom God founds the earth;
by understanding God upholds the heavens;
by God's knowledge the deeps opened up,
and the clouds drop dew.

Proverbs 3:19-20

Spirit of God hover over our unformedness,
Word of God speak wholeness into our unfruitfulness
Source of all being; remake us and renew us by Word and by Spirit.

Pause to open ourselves to God…

Listen! Words of Wisdom, let's focus and take to heart.

Collects, Psalm(s) and readings. There may be a time of quiet and/or shared reflection. A framework for reflection (p.139) may be used.

From the creation of the world, God's eternal power and nature, though invisible, have been perceived and grasped through the things God has made.

Rom.1:20

The following Canticle may be said or some other

You are worthy, our Lord and God,
to receive glory and honour and power,
for you made all things,
by your will everything persists
and was created

Revelation 4:11

The heavens tell out God's glory;
and the skies proclaim God's handiwork.
Day streams data to day,
and night declares knowledge to night.
This is not speech; there are no words;
their voices are not heard;
and yet their forthtelling propagates through the whole earth,
and their words to the world's end.

Psalm 19:1-4

> *We recognise and celebrate God's loving greatness…*

So with angels and atoms,stars and saints, earth and sky and sea.
We hallow your name, joining with the eternal song of heaven
Holy, holy, holy Lord,
God of power and might,
heaven and earth are full of your glory,
hosanna in the highest.

Creator God, release your Spirit to brood over as yet unspent nature and enflourish the the deep viridity[3] of the world.

Send forth your Spirit:
And renew the face of the earth.

Sustainer of all, in the searing of uncaring trade and the smearing of human toil let there grow renewal, justice and peace.

Send forth your Spirit:
And renew the face of the earth.

Loving and reaching-out God, as you touch and woo every heart, let there grow a reverence for all you have made and freedom to respond to your grace.

Send forth your Spirit:
And renew the face of the earth.

> *…prayers or biddings may be added here, the leader ending with:*

Send forth your Spirit:
And renew the face of the earth.

May we know your comfort and provision as we seek your will for life and cosmos

> *…prayers or biddings asking for God's provision may be added here the leader ending with*

Send forth your Spirit:
And renew the face of the earth.

We are debtors to the ecosystem you have provided for our nurture. We have trespassed on the resources you made for others to use.We have abused your hospitality and befouled the earth.

Send your Spirit forth
And renew the face of our lives

We have pointed fingers at others yet refused to be held accountable

Send your Spirit forth
And renew the face of our lives

We are debtors to mercy and heirs of grace. Thank you for bearing our disgrace. We are forgiven in your determination to bless.

Lead us into gracious and merciful living;
generous and respectful in all you have made.
As we contemplate your creation, O God,
we see wildness and order,
chance and necessity,
Freedom and limits.
Grant us to use lovingly our freedoms
to be wise in using the order of things
And wary of our vulnerability to misleadings.
For yours is the kingdom, the power and the glory.
Now and forever, amen

Kingdomtide

Kingdom season is in the few weeks before Advent, presently this means during November. The theme of the Kingdom season is Christ's light being brought to the darkness of the world and life into death. It is a time to remember and take encouragement from the dead in Christ, the saints in light.

The light shines in the darkness,
and the darkness did not overcome it.
The true light enlightens everyone,
and has come into the world.

> *Lights /candles may be lit. A Collect may be said.*

My soul faints with longing for your salvation,
and in your word have I put my hope.

> *Psalms and reading[s]*

The word that goes out from God's mouth shall not return empty,
it shall accomplish God's purpose,
and succeed in what it is sent to do.

> *Reflection individually or together. A framework for reflection ((p.139) available to help if desired.*

> *The following Canticle may be said or some other*

Great and wonderful are your deeds,
Lord God the Almighty.
Just and true are your ways,
O ruler of the nations.
Who shall not revere
and praise your name, O Lord?

For you alone are holy.
All nations shall come
and worship in your presence:
for your just dealings have been revealed.
To the One who sits on the throne
and to the Lamb
be blessing and honour,
glory and might,
for ever and ever. Amen.

Revelation 15:3,4

O Lord, open our lips
And our mouth shall proclaim your praise.
Blessèd are you, Heaven's High King and judge of
all, we give you praise and honour for with you is the
well of life,
In your light we see light.

Praise and thanksgiving, silent or aloud.

God in heaven; father and mother to us,
Hallowed be your name

Your will is for the Light of Christ to illumine
everyone.

May your light shine on all for whom we pray and
chase the shadows from the situations we are
concerned about.

We bring our concerns for people or events to
God, silently or aloud.

In that day, mourning and crying and pain will be no
more and God will wipe away every tear.
Your kingdom Come.

In that day, of the increase of Christ's government and of peace there shall be no end.
Your kingdom Come.
In that day, your Spirit will fill all things and all shall know you.
Your kingdom Come.
In that day, death will be no more;
Your kingdom Come.

...

As we seek to walk in Light, you promise to supply our need

...sharing of needs, silently or aloud ...

Seeking first your righteousness
All things shall be added.

Jesus proclaimed 'The Kingdom of God is at hand, change your outlook and commit yourselves to the Good News'

We pause to recognise what of our life needs to change in the light of God's Reign

When the shadows we have cast have hidden the light for others,
Father forgive.

We reflect on what we may need to forgive

We forgive the shadows others have cast on our lives.
Father forgive.
This we call to mind and therefore we have hope:
The steadfast love of the Lord never ceases,
God's mercies never come to an end:

They are new every morning,
Great is your faithfulness, O Lord:
great is your faithfulness.

Lamentations 3:19 ff

*We reflect on the coming day: it's potential
challenges to our living out the Good News and
recognising it may bring things for which we are
unprepared.*

In all that today may bring; the anticipated and the
surprising,
The pleasant and the testing;
Go before us, alert us to the real issues,
strengthen us for Good,
awaken us if we sleepwalk into sin,
show us the way out of the Darkness
and fill us with love, hope and peace
as we cling fast to you.
Amen.

Magnificat days

Magnificat season can be observed in the second half of August beginning with the feast of the Virgin Mary on 15th. It's not a recognised church season. These prayers may also be suitable for occasions on which Mary, mother of Jesus, is remembered.

A woman in the crowd raised her voice and said to Jesus, 'Blessed is the womb that bore you and the breasts that nursed you!' But Jesus said, 'Blessed rather are those who hear the word of God and obey it!'

Luke 11:27-8

As we hear God's word, Holy Spirit come upon us,
Power of the Most High, overshadow us.
We will treasure these words
and ponder them in our hearts.

> *Collects, Psalm(s) and readings. are announced and read.*

You have come to the help of your servant Israel,
and remembered your promise of mercy,
The promise you made to our forebears,
to Abraham and his children for ever

We consider, in the light of scripture, what God calls us to.

> *Reflection (together with others where possible), silently and/or aloud. A framework for reflection (p.139) may be used.*

Here we are, servants of the Lord;
let it be with us according to your word.

**My soul proclaims your greatness O Lord;
my spirit rejoices in you O God our Saviour,
You have looked with favour on your lowly
servant.
From this day all generations will call us
blessed:
Almighty, you have done great things for us,
and holy is your name.
You have mercy on those who fear you
from generation to generation.
You have shown strength with your arm
and scattered the proud in their conceit,
casting down the mighty from their thrones
and lifting up the lowly.
You have filled the hungry with good things,
and sent the rich away empty.
You have come to the help of your servant Israel,
remembering your promise of mercy,
the promise made to our forebears,
to Abraham and his children forever.**

*Based on the ELLC translation of
Luke 1:46-55.*

My soul magnifies You, Lord,
my spirit rejoices in God my Saviour,
You have looked with favour on this lowly servant.
You have remembered your promise of mercy

*… Songs and/or words of praise and
thanksgiving could be shared here…*

Almighty, you have done great things for us

and holy is your name.

...

Show strength with your arm, O God
**scatter the proud in the imaginations of their
hearts.**
Cast down the mighty from their thrones
and lift up the lowly.

> *Concerns for the world, the church and
> individuals are shared ...*

Fill the hungry with good things
and send the callous rich empty away

> *... we consider what we need to continue serving
> God ...*

Lest we be scattered from God's purposes, brought
down or sent away empty, let us repent, asking and
offering forgiveness.

> *Pause for reflection on forgiving and being
> forgiven.*

Have mercy upon us
According to your promises.
God says to all who repent; 'Do not be afraid, for you
have found favour with God.'

...

Though the Lord be high, he watches over the lowly.

Let's pause to give our coming hours over to God's
guiding and keeping

...

Though we walk in the midst of trouble, O God;
you will preserve us.
You will stretch forth your hand against the fury of
our enemies;
your right hand will save us.
Make good your purpose for us;
your loving-kindness, O Lord, endures for ever
forsake not the work of your hands.
Make good your purpose for us.

Ps. 138:6-8

From this day forward may we be called blessed
**For the Almighty will have done great things for
us.**

Dark times of year

This form of prayer is for use at times of the year when we feel daylight is short and night-time is long. It is most suitable for late Autumn and Winter especially in Kingdomtide and even an alternate service in Advent.

> *As we start, a candle or candles may be lit or carried into the worship space.*

In your word, O Light of the World, we live, move and have our being. As you have lightened our darkness in the past, we ask, Everliving God, for your awakening within: leading us from delusion to truth, and into your righteous way.

Lead us, Source of all Being, Father and Mother to us:
From darkness to light and into your gracious will.
Lead us, Christ, our Friend and our Brother;
From death to eternal life and into your infinite joy;
Lead us, Divine Spirit, empowering Life within
for we seek your enabling touch.

> *Based on a prayer from the*
> *Church of South India*

Reader: The true light that lightens all has come into the world,
In your light may we see light.

> *Collects, Psalm(s) and readings. At the end of the reading[s]:*

Your word O Lord, is a lamp to our feet and a light to our path.

Sustain us according to your promise and we shall live.

There may be a time of quiet and/or shared reflection. A framework for reflection (p.139) may be used.

At the end of the reflection time, we say together the following Canticle or some other

**The people walking in darkness
have seen a great light;
on those living in the land of darkness,
 a light has dawned.
You have enlarged the nation
and increased its joy.
The people have rejoiced before You
as they rejoice at harvest time
For You have shattered their burdensome yoke
and the rod on their shoulders,
the staff of their oppressor,
For a child will be born for us,
a son will be given to us,
and the government will be on His shoulders.
He will be named Wonderful Counsellor,
Mighty God, Eternal Father, Prince of Peace.
The dominion will be vast,
and its prosperity will never end.
He will reign on the throne of David
and over his kingdom,
to establish and sustain it with justice
and righteousness from now on and forever.
The zeal of the Lord of Hosts will accomplish
this.**

O Lord, open our lips
And our mouth shall proclaim your praise.

Blessèd are you, Sovereign God , judge of all, we give you praise and honour for the brightness of your kingdom lightens the darkness of this passing age and you show us the light of your glory in the face of Jesus Christ,

Father in heaven,
Hallowed be your name

> *praise and thanksgiving, silent or aloud.*

You desire the Light of Christ to illumine everyone. May your light shine on all for whom we pray and chase the shadows from the situations we are concerned about.

> *… We bring our concerns for people or events to God, silently or aloud.…*

Your will be done:
Lighten our darkness.

Into the coldness of selfishness and greed bring the warmth of your loving generosity.

Your will be done:
Lighten our darkness.

In times of frustration and lack of growth or development, bring the hope of springtime and redemption.

Your will be done:

Lighten our darkness.

As we seek to walk in Light, you promise to give what we need.

> *… sharing of needs, silently or aloud….*

Seeking first your righteousness
All things shall be added.

Jesus says, "I am the light of the world, whoever comes to me will never walk in darkness but have the light of life."

And yet our thoughts, words or deeds have sometimes revealed darkness

> *We pause to recognise what of our life needs to change in the light of God in Christ*

When the shadows we have cast have hidden the light for others,
Father forgive.
We offer the light of forgiveness for the shadows others have cast on our lives.
Father forgive.
You are the fountain of life;
in your light we see light.
Your word is a lantern to our feet
and a light upon our paths.

Let's call to mind all that today may bring; the anticipated and the surprising. The pleasant and the painful.

> *… We reflect on the coming day…*

When we are tested by temptation

strengthen us.
When our commitment to your Love is put to trial,
save us.
When evil ensnares,
free us.
For yours is the kingdom, the power and the glory,
now and forever. Amen

Prayers before sleep at night

The following prayers are envisaged as being used last thing at night, a kind of prayer nightcap, so to speak. They draw from traditional services of Night Prayer (often known as 'Compline' -using the name of the monastic late-night office). The traditional office uses the Song of Simeon (also known as the Nunc Dimittis) after the reading. These orders of night prayer use it to round-off an initial reflection on the good things of the day and of the things to thank God for. Some of the traditional -and indeed, well-loved, prayers have been incorporated at points appropriate to the flow of the Lord's prayer which is the structuring principle of the orders. Also included is a hymn. The traditional hymn has been rewritten with new verses emphasising different aspects of the Lord's Prayer, and accordingly it is placed at different points in the orders to reflect this. The tune, however, is the same even where the words have changed.

There is an emphasis on ending the day.by reflecting on it with God. The traditional reading in the office of Compline is very short and here the office focuses on prayer rather than a reading from scripture as such though the prayers are heavily drawn from scripture, particularly the Psalms.

The part of the Lord's prayer concerned with daily bread has been taken to be able to include a good night's sleep or rest within its broader meaning. This means that sometimes some of the traditional phrases from Compline have been repurposed within the pattern of prayers to reflect this interpretation.

These do not have particular days or seasons associated with them. You are invited to use the five forms as you wish. Whether that means simply rotating through them day by day or using one over a period of time before then moving on to using another is entirely for you to decide and try out.

Night Prayer One

You have multiplied, O God, your wondrous deeds
and your thoughts toward us;
none can compare with you.
We give thanks to you, O God and tell of your
wondrous deeds.
we give thanks; your name is near.

Psalms 40:5 & 75:1

> *... Pause to reflect on what we have seen of God
> in the past day.*

Now, Lord, you let your servant go in peace:
 your word has been fulfilled.
 My own eyes have seen the salvation
 which you have prepared in the sight of every
people;
 A light to reveal you to the nations
 and the glory of your people Israel.

ELLC Nunc Dimittis.

Hallowed be your name Father, through the Son, in
the Holy Spirit:
As in the beginning; so now; and forever. Amen.

...

Let us pray

> *... pause to recall, and perhaps to share,
> particular concerns before God. ...*
> *(the words to the following may be sung to the
> tune 'Te Lucis' -traditional compline hymn)*

O God with you we rest our cares
 bring good of them in all affairs

And as the world turns on its round
may justice, peace and hope abound.

And as we pause to take our sleep
bring comfort to all those who weep
and work into to the wide world's life
the grace that ends ungodly strife.

O God bring good news to the poor
and make your peacely rule more sure
tread underfoot all ill and woe
So right and health and goodness grow

We lie down and sleep; we wake again, for the Lord
sustains us.

Save us, O Lord, while waking, and guard us
while sleeping, that awake we may watch with
Christ and asleep we may rest in peace.

Search me out, O God, and know my heart; try me
and know my restless thoughts.
Look well whether there be any wickedness in
me.

Psalm 139:23

Pause to recognise wrongness in our lives today;
both what we've caused and what we need to
forgive.

Holy God,
holy and strong,
holy and immortal:
have mercy on us.

Let us attend: God breathes forgiveness on those who confess their sins.

From the darkness of our sins we walk.
lead us in the way that is everlasting.
 Let us hear of your loving-kindness in the morning,
for in you we put our trust;
 show us the way we should walk in,
for we lift up our soul to you.

from Psalm 143

Night Prayer Two

Seek the Lord and his strength; seek his presence
continually.
Remember the wonderful works he has done,
we extol you, O God
and bless your name forever and ever

Psalms 105:4 & 145:1

> *...Pause to reflect on what we have seen of God
> in the past day.*

Now, Lord, you let your servant go in peace:
 your word has been fulfilled.
 My own eyes have seen the salvation
 which you have prepared in the sight of every
people;
 A light to reveal you to the nations
 and the glory of your people Israel.

ELLC Nunc Dimittis.

Hallowed be your name Father, through the Son, in
the Holy Spirit:
As in the beginning; so now; and forever. Amen.

As we lie down to rest we lay before God the
restless world.

Your lore and wisdom infuse the earth
fulfil your heavenly dreams among us.
Thwart ill-will and spiteful imaginings
Let justice, mercy and truth flourish for good.
Extend through your church a welcome to all
And entice the world to the feast of Fulfilment
Knit together Dayspring in the womb of night
Let darkness nurture new hopeful futures.

Further concerns may be expressed …

In peace we will lie down and sleep;
for you alone, Lord, make us dwell in safety

From Psalm 4:8

O God, your unstinting providence sustains the world, our lives, our living: Take care for us, and keep us ever mindful that our common weal flows from each other's toil and care. **Amen.**

Adapted from a prayer in Compline, The Book of Common Prayer, ECUSA, 1979

The following hymn may be sung (Tune: 'Te Lucis' traditional for Compline)

As now our day draws to its close,
we rest from this life's ebbs and flows,
God grant that when we rest this night
disturbances do not alight.

For falling short and wrong things done
we ask forgiveness in your Son
and we do now give up our aims
for recompense and vengeful claims

Search us O God and know our hearts, test us and know our anxious thoughts;
See if there is any offensive way in us.

Psalm 139:23f

Pause to recognise our wrongs of the day…

Have mercy on us, O God, according to your steadfast love;

according to your abundant mercy blot out our transgressions.
Create in us clean hearts, O God,
and put a new and right spirit within us.
Jesus says: come to me all who are weary and burdened and I will give them rest.
Thanks be to God.

See Psalm 51:1 & Matthew 11:28

Into your hands, O Lord, I commend my spirit.
Into your hands, O Lord, I commend my spirit.
 For you have redeemed me, Lord God of truth.
I commend my spirit.
Keep me as the apple of your eye.
Hide me under the shadow of your wings.

Psalm 31:5 and 17:8

Night Prayer Three

We think about all your deeds,
We meditate on the works of your hands.
You, O God, are our fortress,
the God who shows us steadfast love

Psalms 143:5, 59:17

> *... Time to reflect on what we have seen of God in the past day.*

Now, Lord, you let your servant go in peace:
 your word has been fulfilled.
 My own eyes have seen the salvation
 which you have prepared in the sight of every people;
 A light to reveal you to the nations
 and the glory of your people Israel.

ELLC Nunc Dimittis.

Hallowed be your name, Father, through the Son, in the Holy Spirit:
As in the beginning; so now and forever. Amen.
O God, make speed to save us.
O Lord, make haste to help us.
Keep Your people, Lord, in the arms of Your embrace.
Shelter them under Your wings.
Be their light in darkness.
Be their hope in distress.
Be their calm in anxiety.
Be strength in their weakness.
Be their comfort in pain.
Be their song in the night.
Show the wonder of Your great love,

Save by Your right hand those who take refuge in You.

Be present, O merciful God,
 and protect us through the hours of this night,
 so that we who are wearied
by the changes and chances of this life
may rest in your eternal faithfulness;
through Jesus Christ our Lord. **Amen**.

As this day draws to a close for us, we recognise
that there have been occasions when we have
closed off the outworking of God's grace and love in
and through our lives.

...

Hide your face from our sins,
and blot out all our iniquities
Restore to us the joy of your salvation,
and sustain in us a willing spirit.

Psalm 51:12

If we confess our sins, God is faithful and just and
will forgive us our sins and cleanse us from all
unrighteousness.

Lighten our darkness, O Lord, we pray;
and in your great mercy
defend us from all perils and dangers of this night
for the love of your only Son, our Savior Jesus
Christ.
Amen

Night Prayer Four

How abundant is your goodness that you have laid
up for those who fear you,
**and accomplished for those who take refuge in
you,**
I will meditate on all your work,
and muse on your mighty deeds.

Psalm 31:19 & 72:12

> *We reflect on what we have seen of God in the
> past day.*

**Now, Lord, you let your servant go in peace:
your word has been fulfilled.
My own eyes have seen the salvation
which you have prepared in the sight of every
people;
A light to reveal you to the nations
and the glory of your people Israel.**

ELLC Nunc Dimittis.

Hallowed be your name Father, through the Son, in
the Holy Spirit:
As in the beginning; so now; and forever. Amen.

O God of all hopefulness, we pray for the fleshing
out of your dream for your world.
No more shall the sound of weeping be heard in it,
or the cry of distress.
Your kingdom come
your will be done on earth as in heaven
No more shall there be in it an infant that lives but a
few days, or an old person who does not live out a
lifetime.

Your kingdom come
your will be done on earth as in heaven
They shall not labour in vain, or bear children for
calamity.
Your kingdom come
your will be done on earth as in heaven
Isaiah 65:20-23

In peace we will lie down and sleep;
for you alone, Lord, make us dwell in safety

Our refuge and our stronghold, God, in whom we put
our trust. deliver us from the snare of the fowler and
from the deadly pestilence. Cover us with your wings
and make us safe under your feathers; Your
faithfulness shall be our shield and buckler.

We have laboured in vain and lived dreams in
disharmony to God's.

Pause for reflection.

Show us your mercy, O Lord;
And grant us your salvation.
Make our hearts clean, O God;
and renew a right spirit within us.

Be sober, be vigilant, because your adversary the
devil is prowling round like a roaring lion, seeking for
someone to devour. Resist him, strong in the faith.

Hymn (suggested tune: Te Lucis)

O God, our day draws to its close,
we rest from this life's ebbs and flows,
we ask that when we rest this night

disturbances do not alight.

And now we trust, at our day's end,
that you our inward peace defend
and bring us at the new day's start
to waken well and cheered of heart.
Amen.

And so may God + Lover, Beloved and Loving,
sustain us this night, always and ever.

Amen.

Night Prayer Five

Your steadfast love, O Lord, extends to the heavens,
your faithfulness to the clouds
All your works shall give thanks to you, O Lord.
and all your faithful shall bless you.

Psalms 36:5 & 145:10

Pause to reflect on what we have seen of God
over the past day...

Now, Lord, you let your servant go in peace:
your word has been fulfilled.
My own eyes have seen the salvation
which you have prepared in the sight of every
people;
A light to reveal you to the nations
and the glory of your people Israel.

ELLC Nunc Dimittis.

Hallowed be your name Father, through the Son, in
the Holy Spirit:
As in the beginning; so now; and forever. Amen.

Hymn (suggested tune: Te Lucis)

O loving Carer, God of grace
you welcome us with smiling face,
and we may ever rest at peace
for we, to you, our cares release.

O God transform the woes of life
Bring good from ill and peace to strife.
Move greed and pride from seats of power
so justice, mercy, healing flower

And as we pause to take our sleep
bring comfort to all those who weep
and work into to the wide world's life
the grace that ends ungodly strife.

In quietness let us recall those whose lives our lives touch and the cares of the wider world.

A time of quiet reflection and petition...

Our help comes from the Lord
Who made heaven and earth
God keeps us, and will neither slumber or sleep
The Everliving will watch over our life.
God, be mindful of our coming and going
Now and forevermore.

Psalm 121

Two things we ask of you, Lord; Keep falsehood and lies afar; give us neither poverty nor riches, but give us simply our daily bread.
See Proverbs 30:7-9

... Pause to recollect our needs before God.

It is in vain that we rise up early and go late to rest, eating the bread of anxious toil; for God gives sleep to those who are beloved.

Let us recognise where we have not welcomed God to be with us or where we have perpetuated unforgiveness.

Pause to recognise wrongness in our lives today; both what we've caused and what we need to forgive...

Send us your Spirit
And renew the face of our lives.
Make our hearts clean, O God
And remake a right spirit within us.
Let us attend; Christ breathes upon us the peace
and forgiveness of God.

Visit this place, O Lord, and drive far from it all
snares of the enemy; let your holy angels dwell with
us to preserve us in peace; and let your blessing be
upon us always; through Jesus Christ our Lord.
Amen.

Amen

A framework for reflection...

...using the pattern of the Lord's prayer

You can use these questions as a way to reflect on the readings in a way that links the reflection to the pattern of the Lord's prayer.

Questions to ask ourselves having read the passages.

-What in these passages speaks to us of who God is, reminds us of some facet of God's greatness or our thankfulness to God?

-Is there something here to inspire us, challenge us or to help us to intercede and/or to work for God's will to be more fully seen here and now on earth?

-Are we reminded of anything that we need from God to continue as faithful followers of Christ?

-Does what we have read highlight anything in our own lives that we need to seek God's mercy for? Does it make us aware of anything we need to let go of or forgive?

-Are we put in mind of one of our weaknesses? Does the passage suggest something that may help us as we face pressures to wander off spiritually?

These questions are offered more as a way to get you started rather than being definitive. You may come up with variant questions or further questions along the same sort of lines. The idea is simply to use the motifs of each section of the Lord's Prayer as a way to think about the passage before you and from there, perhaps to inform your prayer.

Canticles

This is a collection of canticles used in this book. 'Canticles' is a word used to label portions of the Bible which are traditionally used in prayer together in daily offices. These 'little songs' (which is what the word roughly means) are often presented as songs or poetry in scripture. Sometimes the term is used of poems or prose pieces which are like the scriptural canticles but not actually found in the Bible or the Apocrypha.

This collection is gathered in this place to make it easier for you to find other canticles if you want to use them instead of ones set within the texts of the offices in the book. Some of those in this section are not found in the daily or seasonal prayer-forms. To get back to where you were, it is probably easiest to use the 'back' button on your e-reader.

The following are all printed in bold to remind us that the default for group-prayer is to say them together. However, they could be said back and forth using alternate lines or each person taking a line or in some other way.

Each of these can be followed by this form of words:
Hallowed be your name Father,
through the Son,
in the Holy Spirit:
As in the beginning;
so now; and forever. Amen.

That is a version of a traditional doxology:
Glory to the Father and to the Son and to The Holy
Spirit; as it was in the beginning, is now and shall be
forever. Amen.

The "Hallowed be..." version is an attempt to present
it in a way that preserves the Father-centred focus of
the Lord's prayer. It is not meant in any way to
indicate a disagreement with the doctrine of the
Trinity.

The Benedictus, "The Song of Zechariah"

*"Benedictus" is from the Latin word for 'blessed' which is
the first word in the canticle. This version has been
changed slightly from the contemporary English one most
contemporary prayer books would use. It has been
change in form so as to directly address God as 'you'
rather than referring to God less directly as 'he' and 'him'.
A couple of lines which are an aside to the Christ Child in
the original text in Luke chapter 2, have also been omitted.*

**Blessed are you, Lord God of Israel;
you have come to your people and set us free.
You have raised up for us a mighty Saviour,
born of the house of your servant David.
Through your holy prophets you promised of old
to save us from our enemies,
from the hands of all who hate us;
to show mercy to our forebears
and to remember your holy covenant.**

This was the oath you swore to our father Abraham:
to set us free from the hands of our enemies,
free to worship you without fear,
holy and righteous before you, all the days of our life.
In your tender compassion, O God
the dawn from on high shall break upon us,
to shine on those who dwell in darkness and the shadow of death,
and to guide our feet into the way of peace.

Based on the English translation of the Benedictus copyright © 1988, by the English Language Liturgical Consultation..

The Magnificat: "The Song of Mary"

"Magnificat" is the first word in the Latin version of this canticle and means 'magnifies' or 'proclaims the greatness of'. This version of the canticle has been changed slightly from the contemporary English one most contemporary prayer books would use. It has been change in form so as to directly address God as 'you' rather than as 'he' and 'him'.

My soul proclaims your greatness O Lord;
my spirit rejoices in you O God our Saviour,
You have looked with favour on your lowly servant.
From this day all generations will call us blessed:

Almighty, you have done great things for us,
and holy is your name.
You have mercy on those who fear you
from generation to generation.
You have shown strength with your arm
and scattered the proud in their conceit,
casting down the mighty from their thrones
and lifting up the lowly.
You have filled the hungry with good things,
and sent the rich away empty.
You have come to the help of your servant Israel,
remembering your promise of mercy,
the promise made to our forebears,
to Abraham and his children forever.

*Based on the English translation
of the Magnificat -The Song of
Mary, Luke 1:46-55- copyright ©
1988, by the English Language
Liturgical Consultation.*

The Song of Simeon:."Nunc Dimittis"

"Nunc Dimittis" comes from the first two words in the Latin version of this canticle and means, roughly, 'Now let leave'. Traditionally it is used in Night prayer and on the Feast of the Presentation in the Temple ("Candlemas") when Simeon's prophecy over the infant Christ is recalled.

**Now, Lord, you let your servant go in peace:
your word has been fulfilled.
My own eyes have seen the salvation
which you have prepared in the sight of every people;
A light to reveal you to the nations
and the glory of your people Israel.**

The Message of the Cross

This is not a traditional canticle, but it has some of the character of one and some may like to use it at various times.

**The message of the cross is foolishness to those who are perishing,
but to us who are being saved it is the power of God.**

For since, in the wisdom of God, the world did not know God through wisdom,
God decided, through the foolishness of our proclamation,
to save those who believe.
For some demand signs and others desire wisdom,
but we proclaim Christ crucified,
a stumbling-block to some and foolishness to others.
But to those who are the called,
Christ is the power of God
and the wisdom of God.
For God's foolishness is wiser than human wisdom,
and God's weakness is stronger than human strength.

From 1 Corinthians 1:18-25

What we have received

What we have received
is not the spirit of the world,
but the Spirit who is from God,
so that we may understand
what God has freely given us.
No one can say, "Jesus is Lord,"
except by the Holy Spirit.

1Cor 12:3b

The Song of Christ's Glory

Though in the form of God,
Christ did not regard equality with God as
something to be held.
He emptied himself, taking on the form of a
slave.
Jesus was born in human likeness;
and found in human form.
He humbled himself
and was obedient into death
even death on a cross.
Therefore, God highly exalted Christ
giving the name above every name.
So at the name of Jesus
every knee should bow,
in heaven and on earth and under the earth,
and every tongue confess that Jesus Christ is
Lord,
to the glory of God the Father.

from Philippians 2

A Song of the Cosmic Christ

Jesus Christ is the image of the invisible God,
the firstborn over all creation.
For in Christ all things were created:
things in heaven and on earth,
visible and invisible,
whether thrones or powers or rulers or
authorities;

all things have been created through him and for
him.
He is before all things,
and in him all things hold together.
And he is the head of the body, the church;
he is the beginning and the firstborn from among
the dead,
so that in everything he might have the
supremacy.
For God was pleased to have all his fullness
dwell in him,
and through him to reconcile to himself all
things,
whether things on earth or things in heaven,
by making peace through his blood, shed on the
cross.

From Colossians 1:16ff

You are Worthy

You are worthy, our Lord and God,
to receive glory and honour and power,
for you made all things,
by your will everything persists
and was created

Rev.4:11

Great and Wonderful

Great and Wonderful are your deeds, Lord God
the Almighty.
Just and true are your ways, O ruler of the
nations.
Who shall not revere and praise your name, O
Lord?
For you alone are holy.
All nations shall come and worship in your
presence:
for your just dealings have been revealed.
To the One who sits on the throne and to the
Lamb
be blessing and honour and glory and might, for
ever and ever.
Amen.

Revelation 15.3,4

Canticle of Solomon

Blessed are you,
O God of our ancestor Israel
for ever and ever.
Yours, O Lord, are the greatness,
the power, the glory,
the victory, and the majesty;
for all that is in the heavens
and on the earth is yours;
yours is the kingdom, O Lord,
and you are exalted as head above all.

1 Chronicles 29:10-11

A Canticle of Salvation

The people walking in darkness have seen a
great light;
on those living in the land of darkness, a light
has dawned.
You have enlarged the nation
and increased its joy.
The people have rejoiced before You
as they rejoice at harvest time
For You have shattered their burdensome yoke
and the rod on their shoulders,
the staff of their oppressor,
For a child will be born for us,
a son will be given to us,
and the government will be on His shoulders.
He will be named Wonderful Counsellor,
Mighty God,
Eternal Father,
Prince of Peace.
The dominion will be vast,
and its prosperity will never end.
He will reign on the throne of David
and over his kingdom,
to establish and sustain it with justice and
righteousness
from now on and forever.
The zeal of the Lord of Hosts will accomplish
this.

Excerpted from Isaiah 9.2-7

A Canticle of God's Word.

O God, Your thoughts are not our thoughts,
nor are our ways your ways, O Lord.
For as the heavens are higher than the earth,
so are your ways higher than our ways
and your thoughts than our thoughts.
For as the rain and the snow come down from
heaven,
and do not return there until they have watered
the earth,
making it bring forth and sprout,
giving seed to the sower and bread to the eater,
so shall your word be that goes out from your
mouth;
it shall not return to you empty,
it shall accomplish what you purpose,
and succeed in what you sent it for.
For we shall go out in joy,
and be led back in peace;
the mountains and the hills shall burst into song,
and all the trees of the field shall clap their
hands.

see Isaiah 55.8-12

A Song of Ezekiel

You take us from the nations,
you gather us from every land,
You sprinkle clean water upon us,
and wash us from all our uncleannesses,

as from all our idols you cleanse us.
A new heart you give us,
a new spirit you put within us.
You remove from our body the heart of stone
and give a heart of flesh.
we are your people,
and you are our God.

based on Ezekiel 36.24-26,28b

Collects

The following are provided for use when access to collects from other sources is not possible. These collects are composed or refashioned by Jeremy Clines from older collects used by the Church of England. This is a short selection of collects that I think might be helpful for occasional use.

Collects are designed to 'collect' together people's thoughts and prayers at one particular point in time. They have a normal structure of addressing God by recognising some divine quality and on the basis of that quality they then ask God for something, ending with some further recognition of God's qualities.

....

O Creator, from who all good things come,
grant to us your humble servants,
that we may see you in all your works.
Inspire us to think on your goodness,
and be guided to become holy stewards
in the creation, which holds together
in Jesus Christ our Lord.
Amen.

Holy God,
faithful and unchanging:
enlarge our minds with the knowledge
of your world, your cosmos and your truth.
Draw us more deeply into the mystery of your love.
Help us truly serve and worship you,

Father, Son and Holy Spirit,
one God, now and forever.
Amen.

All-loving God,
in your service we receive perfect freedom.
Show us your purposes for our lives
here on earth that we may obey you
with all our heart and mind and strength,
through Jesus Christ our redeemer.
Amen.

God of mercy,
in giving us yourself in Jesus the Christ,
as the bread of life,
we live in the hope of life without hunger.
As we serve you and the world you created,
may we who eat, be bread to others,
may we who drink, pour out your love.
Amen.

Eternal God,
in Jesus, the Christ,
you served, among the crowds,
and you were with the wild animals,
and angels served you.
Equip us to be givers and receives of that same
love and hospitality; in the church, and with
the peoples and creatures of our world.

Help us notice your presence in others
and in our own lives.
Amen.

God, whose Spirit hovers over
the deep chaos, bringing order;
by your self-giving grace
we can find your love
and desire to see your promises fulfilled
for ourselves, humanity and whole earth.
Help us share your vision for your world
both now and in the new creation.
Through Jesus Christ our rescuer and redeemer.
Amen.

Go with us, God, into our lives
and our world, guiding our feet,
thoughts, hopes and our actions.
May your continual help equip
us to serve your divine purpose
for our world and our lives,
both now and for ever,
through Jesus Christ our rescuer.
Amen.

God who angels and animals worship;
you equip us with new hope,
and empower us with your Spirit.
Help us work with you to

protect and restore the broken
and forgotten people and places of our world,
through Jesus Christ our redeemer.
Amen.

All-powerful God,
you showed us
in rising from death
the promise of eternity.
Encourage us to view
our lives and world within
your all-loving and eternal nature.
Amen.

God our creator, in Christ
we see your love for our world
is stronger than death or despair.
Gift us with faith to trust your rescue.
Gift us with hope for creation's liberation.
Gift us with love for our journey towards you.
Amen.

God, you love the world.
Your rule of peace was revealed
in Jesus, before he suffered and
died by the rule of law.
Help us see how much stronger
your love is than death.
Strengthen us so we may

serve you in this world,
even when love may mean that we suffer.
Amen.

Creator God,
in Christ you make all things new.
With creation, we long for freedom.
Come and renew our lives and our world,
with your grace and love.
Help us notice such gifts of hope,
so we may point out the signs of
eternal recovery, close at hand.
Amen.

For more of these collects which have particular
connection with Christian environmental concerns,
go to Jeremy Clines' website at
http://latequartet.blogspot.co.uk/.

Acknowledgments

I gratefully acknowledge the help of various people
who have prayed these prayers with me and have
given ideas and comments in the development of
them. I'm sorry to say that in over 20 years of
developing these offices, (at first only for my own
use), I haven't keep a record of who they all are.

Please know that if you are one of them, I am grateful for your fellowship and your time as well as any comments or reactions that have helped me to revise and edit the collection over the years. There are a number of people who kindly responded to my request to pray them in more or less the form that they are found in this book and to offer any comments and suggestions. So thanks therefore to the following people for beta testing at least some of the offices in this book.

Martin Poole; Mandy Thorlby; Andy Lie Stephen Kaye; Andy Lord; Laura Schofield; Andrew Dowsett; Michael Leyden; Sally Nash; Rachel Hudson; Catherine Lack; Rachel Morris; Diane Kutar; Glyn Evans; Suzanne Vernon-Yorke; Sal Bateman; Alice Snowden;Tracy Voysey; Indy Sartech; Christine Ainsley; Leigh Greenwood; Eileen Ross; Elliot Swattridge; Olivia Davidson; Janet Frymann; Marga Burke-Lowe; Christine Sine; John Grice; Karenza Passmore; Becky Allon-Smith; Elaine Ryder; Marika Rose;Tracy Reynolds, Naomi Allen; Susan Farmer; Val Thomas; Mark Pierson; Darren Koh; Colin Blake; Shaeron Caton-Rose; Clive Barrett; Rob Hawkins; Lesley Shuker; Chris Bainbridge; Cheryl (Lyn) May; Lis Burke; Katrina Martin Gredoña; Dana Delap; Jo Tatum; Lorna Bryan; Alan Gregory; Andrew Holmes; Jim Craig; Eileen Turner; Helen Scott; John Bentham; Sian Yates. Thanks are also due to Jeremy Clines for permission to use some of his collects.

A first stage of these liturgies brought together both the daily offices and the pattern of the Lord's Prayer. That stage can be found towards the end of my 2005 book *Praying the Pattern*. Thanks are due to the various people who have prayed some and parts of those prayers with me. You know who you are!

Bible versions used

Many of the prayers are drawn from scripture. The following versions have been used within the terms of their copyright licenses.

New Revised Standard Version Bible: Anglicised Edition, copyright © 1989, 1995 The Division of Christian Education of the National Council of the Churches of Christ in the United States of America. Used by permission, all rights reserved.

The Holy Bible, New International Version® Anglicized, NIV® Copyright© 1979, 1984, 2011 by Biblica, Inc.® Used by permission. All rights reserved worldwide.

It is not infrequently the case that the wording of the small portions of scripture that I have used at various points are pretty much the same across two or more versions. To further muddy the waters, it is worth noting that I have sometimes reworked the phrases myself, using the Greek NT where appropriate.

Liturgical texts

In the course of collecting, writing, praying, re-writing and amending it has been hard to keep track of the minutiae of sources. I hope that I have managed to acknowledge the sources of major influence and of larger phrases in prayers. I would be happy to acknowledge further things that may be brought to my attention.

A small number of texts are produced by the English Language Liturgical Consultation which has produced a number of texts for use ecumenically. Some of their canticles are used in this book under the terms of their licence as follows:

English translations of Gloria Patri, Nunc Dimittis, Magnificat and Benedictus © 1988 English Language Liturgical Consultation (ELLC). www.englishtexts.org . Used by permission.

However, it should be noted that the Magnificat and Benedictus used in this book have been amended to second-person rather than the original third-person forms of pronouns and verbs and a small section from the Benedictus has been omitted.

Other existing liturgical texts have influenced choices of words, form or format or provided phrases in this collection. These are the various liturgies of the Church of England since 1980, The Northumbria Community's Celtic Daily Prayer, David Adam's The Edge of Glory and The Rhythm of Life: Morning Midday, Evening and Night Liturgies for each Day of

the Week. The Iona Community's Wee Worship
Book.The Society of St Francis's Celebrating
Common Prayer.

Bibliography of Sources used

A wee worship book. Glasgow: Wild Goose
Publications, 2010.

Adam, David. *The edge of glory: prayers in the
Celtic tradition*. Wilton, CT: Morehouse-Barlow,
1988.

Adam, David. *The rhythm of life: Celtic daily prayer*.
London: SPCK, 2008.

Bowsher, Andii. *Praying the pattern: the Lords
prayer as framework for prayer and life*. Great
Britain: Ad Lib, 2005.

Common worship. London: Church House
Publishing, 2006.

Common worship: daily prayer. London: Church
House Publishing, 2015.

Patterns for worship. London: Church House
Publishing, 1995.

Sutheran, Jill, ed. *Celtic daily prayer*. Northumbrian
community. Hetton Hall, Chatton, Northumberland:
Northumbria Community Trust, 1999.

The Church of South India: *Book of common
worship*. Chennai, India: Church of South India,
2006.

Trendell, David. *Celebrating common prayer*.
London: Mowbray, 1995.

Endnotes

 A Lectionary is a document which has a scheme of readings in it. Usually they are from the Bible, though some can include readings from other sources. The idea is that over the course of time, usually a year, the scheme takes the community of readers through a varied diet of Scripture readings. Sometimes these are linked to particular themes or parts of the year and its celebrations or remembrances. Usually the scheme of readings reads books of the bible in sequence. The lectionary referenced here is based on the Revised Common Lectionary which is agreed in basic form by the majority of Christian Churches globally. If you followed the Morning or Evening prayer readings consistently over two years (or one if you were following both) you would have read nearly all of the Bible, only having missed a few things like some genealogies.

[2] Often the Hebrew Scriptures talk of Torah and this is translated 'Law'. Here I have used the word 'Lore' as this captures a more organic, personal-growth and wisdom-related sense that is often present in the Hebrew contrasting our tendency, in the West, to hear 'law' in a legalistic sort of way.

[3] Viridity is a term from Hildegaard of Bingen, a medieval mystic, writer and artist who led a convent. It comes from the Latin for 'greenness' and so captures nature's sign of health and growth.